THE Curriculum for Creativity

MW01351195

ARTistic Pursuits®

MIDDLE SCHOOL 6-8
BOOK TWO

Color and Composition

Brenda Ellis

A Comprehensive Art Program Designed to Involve the Student in the Creative Process While Developing Observational Skills

Newly Expanded Edition

Art Instruction

PLUS Master Works Featuring World Art

Middle School 6-8 Book Two
Color and Composition

Written by Brenda Ellis
Developed by Brenda Ellis and Daniel D. Ellis
Edited by Daniel D. Ellis
Cover, Book Design, Creative Cory, Technique and Project pages illustrated by Brenda Ellis
Student artists are acknowledged beside their works as they appear in the text.

Third Edition

ACKNOWLEDGMENTS

Many thanks go to my husband, Daniel Ellis, for his part in developing this curriculum. Thanks to Christine Ann Feorino for her suggestions and editing in the first edition. Thanks to the students who participated in the lessons and to those who let us share their work with others through this book. Thanks to Dover Publications Inc., NY and Art Resources, NY for supplying the fine art images by the great masters.

Printed in the U.S.A.
ISBN 978-1-939394-07-1

Published by
Artistic Pursuits Inc.
Northglenn, Colorado
www.artisticpursuits.com
alltheanswers@artisticpursuits.com

CONTENTS

ART SUPPLIES

1 – Nupastel assorted colors, set of 24or larger

1 – Sakura Cray Pas Junior Artist Oil Pastel, set of 50

1 – Pastel paper pad in assorted colors

1 – Drawing paper pad (white)

1 – Paper stump

1 – Kneaded eraser

1- Vinyl eraser

1- sharpener

1- Natural Chamois 4x 4in.

Additional supplies: aerosol hairspray (for use as a fixative), masking tape, cotton ball, drawing board (optional)

What Parents Want to Know
Book Content and Scheduling

To learn to make art in color artists have always focused on two groups of topics known as the elements of art, including color theory, and principles of design (composition). Each unit in this book introduces one of these topics over four lessons. Each topic is explored in unique ways, giving students enough experience with the topic that they naturally incorporate it into the way that they draw. It becomes part of their thinking as they draw any kind of subject matter. This kind of focus and many opportunities to practice is how children learn to draw.

First Lesson of Each Unit
Building a Visual Vocabulary

Here students are given a topic to focus on explained in words and pictures. The creative exploration assignment guides students to observe the topic in their own environment. They make connections to real-world experiences, and create a work of art from their own observations and ideas. The assignment for this lesson is colored brown.

Second Lesson of Each Unit
Art Appreciation and Art History

Students see how the topic is used in a work of art by the masters and apply their new observations to a work of art that they create. Students gain knowledge of artists and art history. The assignment for this lesson is colored brown.

Third Lesson of Each Unit
Techniques

Students learn how to use the materials and tools of art and apply that knowledge to make an original work of art. The assignment for this lesson is colored brown.

Fourth Lesson of Each Unit
Application

Students do a final project incorporating new techniques and application of the topic while using a variety of references such as still life objects, landscapes, portraiture, photographs and more! The assignment for this lesson is colored brown.

Scheduling Art Class

CLASSES PER WEEK: TWO   TIME PER CLASS: ABOUT ONE HOUR
PERIOD: 36 WEEKS OR FULL SCHOOL YEAR

This schedule can be modified to fit yours. Keep in mind that students can work independently so it is their time you are scheduling, not your own. Schedule art class at a time when they can complete the art assignment, even if it runs over an hour. Once interrupted, students can rarely return to an activity with as much enthusiasm as they first had. Time for completing each activity will vary greatly depending on students' approaches; however, you should see that as they learn to use more of the elements within their pictures that they are taking more time on each piece.

What Students Want to Know

THE MYSTERIOUS LANGUAGE OF COLOR

If the secrets of color were contained in a book, would you open it? We hope your answer is YES! Just as learning the rules of a sport adds to your enjoyment of playing it, learning the rules of color adds to your enjoyment of making art in color. The first thing everyone should know is where to find the rulebook for color. The rulebook is the color wheel.

1. Learn the rules of color using the color wheel.

"OK", you say, "I'm looking at the color wheel and I don't see any rules." We won't let you be stuck there. Each unit in this book will introduce you to the vocabulary of the color wheel. As you practice one idea at a time, you will soon understand how to mix any colors you want with the few that are in your color set. The second and most important secret when dealing with color is all about what set you choose. Choose a set that contains blue, red, and yellow as shown on the color wheel. Most sets that are designed for students will contain the primary colors that you need.

2. See color variations and color mixtures.

Your brain is a storehouse of color knowledge. You would agree that oranges are orange and lemons are yellow. Each statement has simplified what we really see in order to reduce it to one color for easy identification. What we really see are reflections, shadows, color combinations, and all kinds of other factors that change the original color. Artists learn to see these color variations and color mixtures. An orange may appear blue in the shadows. A lemon may appear green around the ends.

3. Exaggerate colors

Artists may overstep the bounds of truth when applying color to the paper. They do this in order to make objects clearer and easier to identify. They might exaggerate to create a mood. They might use color for its associated meanings by using red because it seems "hot" or green because it seems "peaceful". By using the color rules, you will unlock the secrets of color and gain the skills to work in color with confidence.

COLOR PASTELS

Pastels come in a variety of forms. In this book, you will use hard pastels, which resemble chalk, and oil pastels, which are water resistant. Pastels are pure pigment. The particles are held together with a binder. The first pastels consisted of earth colors. They were used for sketching as pencils are used today. In the 19th century a new source of colors were developed and introduced, adding brighter colors to the pastel group.

Nupastels are harder and denser than soft pastels. Because of this, they are better for drawing thin lines and holding details. They are less dusty; and therefore, much safer to use. Oil pastels create no dust and are very safe to use.

SAFE HANDLING

Handle pastels with care by following the guidelines below. This will be especially important if you decide to progress to professional artist's soft pastels in the future. Forming good habits now will ensure safe handling in the future. The danger when using pastels is created by absorbing the powder, or pigment into the body through the eyes, nose, mouth, or cuts in the skin. Problems associated with the use of pigments do not arise with short-term exposure but many pigments are considered unsafe when handled improperly over time. Following these simple rules of handling will ensure everyone's well being.

DO NOT EAT YOUR PASTELS:

- Do not eat food while drawing or draw near a place where food is prepared. Wash hands thoroughly after drawing with pastels and before eating.
- Do not rub eyes, nose, or bite fingernails when using pastels.
- Keep the dust contained to one area and clean up by vacuuming or wiping the surface of tables or chairs, etc., when finished.
- Do not put a pastel in or near the mouth to wet it.
- Keep all artists materials away from younger siblings, who may put these colorful objects in their mouths.

FIXATIVES

A fixative is a liquid sprayed onto a picture to hold the powdered pigments onto the paper. We suggest that all students use aerosol hairspray to fix the pastel to the paper. It is applied to the paper as one would apply it to the hair by shaking the can, holding it about 12 inches from the paper surface, and spraying a light mist. If using a commercial fixative we caution you to read the label carefully. Commercial fixatives are one of the most dangerous art supply products on the market and one of the most frequently misused. The requirement for adequate ventilation means moving air, the kind found outdoors. Adequate ventilation does not occur by opening a door or window! If you can smell the fumes, you are breathing in toxic vapors. For now, be safe, and use regular hairspray.

UNIT 1
hue
AND INTENSITY

Hue refers to a color by name as in yellow, red, or blue. The words "hue" and "color" are interchangeable.

Intensity refers to the hue's brightness or strength.

All hues on the color wheel are equally intense.

Be Creative

Discovery consists of looking at the same thing as everyone else and thinking something different.
                    -Albert Szent-Gyorgyi, Nobel Prize Winning Physician

Where does your family take vacations? Sometimes we travel to a fantasy world such as a theme park, but people often choose vacations that allow them to get closer to nature. Oceans, lakes, mountains, and the Grand Canyon have always attracted people. When one takes time to be in a natural setting, a connection is made to something more beautiful or more powerful than the manufactured structures of a city landscape.

TRY IT: Take a one-hour vacation. Get away from your usual setting and relax in a spot that is not man-made. It could be a park or meadow. After absorbing the surrounding smells, sights, and sounds, draw your observations using hard pastels. Refer to page five before you use pastels for the first time.

OBJECTIVE: to experience nature; to gather new visual information; to create from personal experience.

CREATIVE CORY

So he's drawing instead of fishing. At least he's using those new waders.

Look at Hue in Art

Every color or hue has a natural intensity, which refers to its brightness or strength. In this work of art by Paul Gauguin, the red cello stands out. The instrument was probably made of a red colored wood, but Gauguin has intensified the color. It stands out against the blue suit of the musician. The yellow color of his skin stands out because of the dark hues of brown and green around him.

PRIMARY COLORS

Paul Gauguin, *Upaupa Schneklud*, 1894. Photo Credit: Dover Publications Inc.

Notice the use of the hues
yellow,
blue,
and red within this painting.

These are called primary colors and are the first colors on the color wheel. They can be mixed to get other colors or used as we see them on the color wheel. Here Gauguin uses the blue and red at full intensity, and lowers the intensity of the yellow.

The Artist

Paul Gauguin (1848-1903)
French Post Impressionist Painter

Paul Gauguin studied with the Impressionist painter, Camille Pissarro. Like the Impressionists, Gauguin used intense hues without giving much attention to form. Unlike the Impressionists, he used flat areas of bright color. Gauguin painted in France and Brittany but soon sought inspiration in Tahiti. He painted the native people. It was the perfect place to find the bright, warm, and pure colors he preferred using.

The Challenge

You will use hard pastels in the first eight units of this book. There are other forms of pastels available that are similar and can be used with hard pastels. Soft pastels, which look much like hard pastels can be used with them. Pastel pencils can be used since they are the same material. Pastel pencils are good for line work, but have a limited color range. They need to be sharpened carefully with a blade because the pastel center breaks easily, so we do not suggest their use in this book.

The end of the hard pastel is a square, allowing several ways of making marks. In the illustration at the left, you can see how the pastel touches the surface of the yellow paper. Use the corner edge for fine line work. Use the flat edge for wider, textural marks. Use the side of the stick for covering large areas.

The Culture
THE HISTORY OF HUES

Hues (colors) are made from pigments (ground up color material). The powdered particles of color are suspended in a binder, which could be made of oils or anything that binds the particles together and makes them usable. The history of hues (color) is a progression of discoveries and invention. When browsing through art history books, one notices a big change in the way color was used before and after the 19th century. In ancient times, people were dependent on the colors found in the earth. Earth or mineral colors used by the earliest cave painters consisted of red, black, and yellow. Black was made from carbon, (charcoal) while reds and yellows were mined from the earth. Like the cave painters, late medieval and Renaissance artists used natural colors made from mineral pigments. "Dug right out of the earth and shaped into sticks with knives, these chalks were ready for drawing. Natural red chalks, with their rich, warm color, were popular from about 1500 to 1900." Michelangelo and Rembrandt used them. The invention of new pigments, produced during the 1800s, gave artists brighter hues. Chemically produced hues led to much excitement about color. Impressionists and those who followed experimented with bold, unnatural colors when painting subjects. Today both mineral hues (mined from the earth) and synthetic hues (chemically manufactured) are available to the artist.

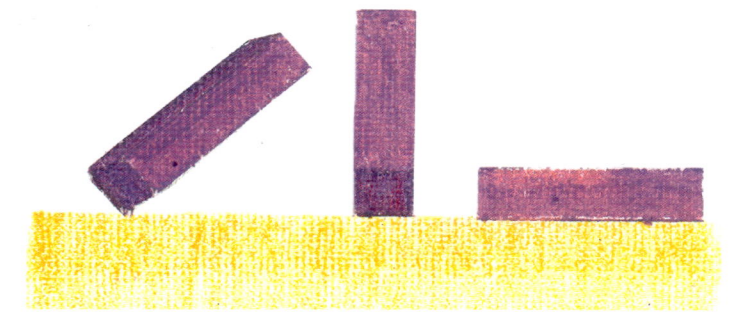

Draw a picture using each side of a pastel stick as shown above. See page nine for an example of the types of marks each side makes.

HOW TO USE PASTELS

It may surprise you that the first thing most pastel artists do when they get new pastels is to break them. That is because holding pastels at different angles allows the artist to use different width strokes.

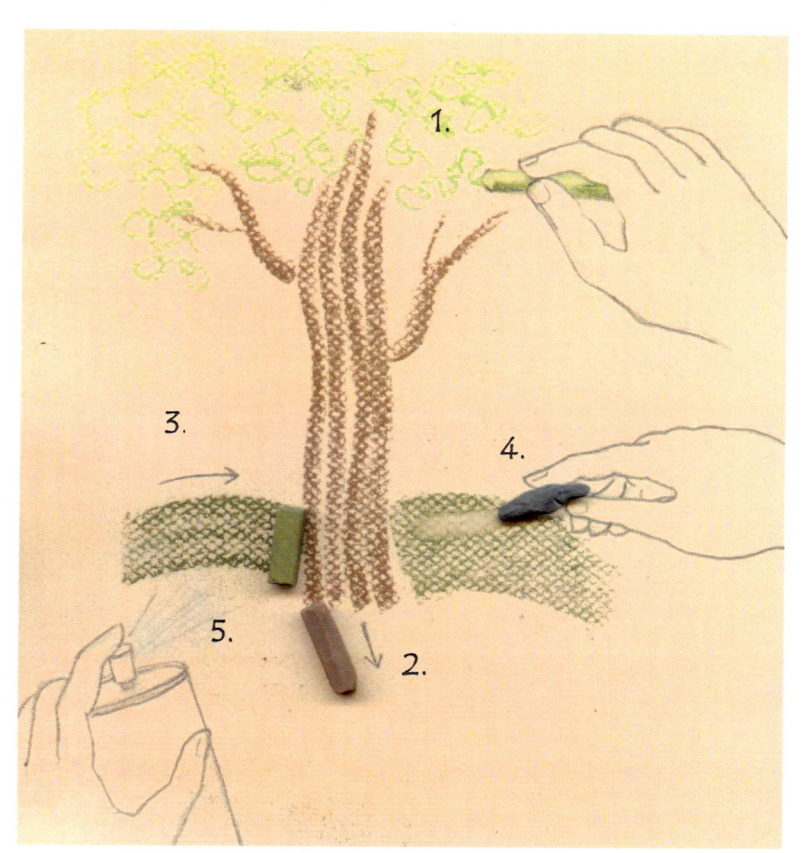

1. Use the point of the stick to make thin marks. 2. Use the blunt end to make medium sized marks. 3. Drag the broad side of the pastel across the paper to make thick marks. Break the stick in half for better control of this technique.
4. Lift pastel from the paper with a kneaded eraser. Knead your kneaded eraser by pulling it apart and folding it on top of itself over again until it becomes soft and pliable. Squeeze it to any shape you need to pick up thin areas or thick. To lift pigment, drag the kneaded eraser across the area several times. 5. When your work is finished, apply fixative (hairspray) to the paper. After shaking the can of aerosol hairspray, spray a light mist onto the artwork. Hold the can about 12 inches from the surface. It is better to give the artwork several light applications rather than a heavy one. The paper will curl immediately, but will flatten again when completely dry.

Try New Techniques

Practice the thin, wide, and thick strokes shown above. Use the kneaded eraser to see how well it erases different colors in your set. Draw a picture of any subject you like. Apply fixative (hairspray) to the paper when finished. Don't worry about results. Right now, just become familiar with handling the edges of the pastel and always finish each pastel work with hairspray.

The Project

Make a drawing using one color. **1.** Start the drawing using the point of the square pastel stick just as you would use a pencil. Some find it easier to hold the pastel stick under the hand as shown. **2.** Instead of erasing mistakes, get rid of lines you don't want by blending them into the paper, using a cotton ball. Draw over the area with lines again. **3.** Use a kneaded eraser to lift pastel off the paper. White marks were made with the eraser to indicate feather patterns on the back and wings of the bird.

1.

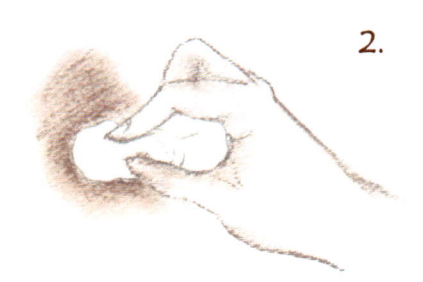

2.

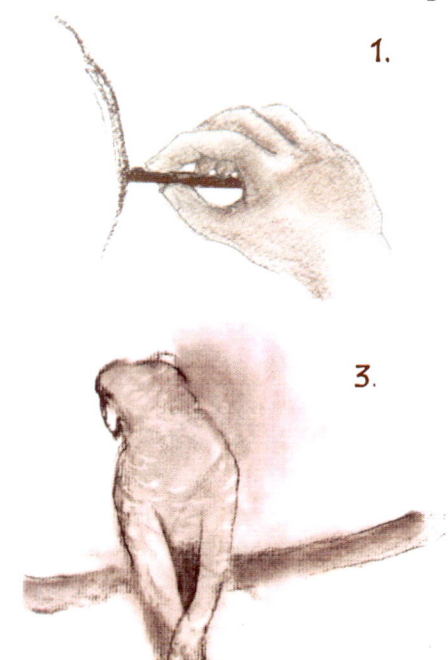

3.

Materials

- hard pastels
- kneaded eraser
- cotton ball
- white paper
- aerosol hairspray

References

Chose a subject that is interesting to you. Pets make great subjects. If you have one, observe the pet directly. If you do not have a pet, work from a photograph. Subjects could be a:

- bird
- cat
- dog
- fish
- reptiles

Student Gallery

Student work below is by Eric Abeyta.

> LOOK BACK! Did you use techniques shown on this page or the previous page?

The Elements Combined: Smooth and Rough Textures

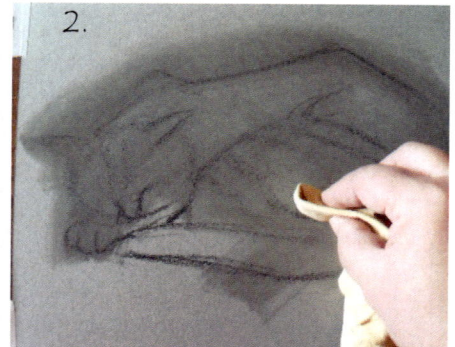

1. Tape paper to the table or drawing board surface so that it does not slide. Draw an outline.

2. Rub out first lines with a chamois and redraw to make corrections.

3. Add dark broad areas with the side of the pastel.

4. Add lightest areas with white or off white pastel.

5. Use the side of the pastel to cover large areas such as the background. In the final work, you see both smooth surfaces created by the chamois on the floor and rough surfaces of pastel over a rough paper on the wall.

UNIT 2
primary and secondary

The primary colors are yellow, red, and blue. When two primary colors are mixed together, they make a secondary color, orange, green, or violet. The color wheel shows the secondary colors between the two primary colors they are made of. In the diagram, P stands for primary color and S stands for secondary color.

Any color in between a primary and secondary is a mixture of the two and called an intermediate color. The color names for intermediate hues are yellow-orange, red-orange, red-violet, blue-violet, blue-green, and yellow-green.

Primary and Secondary colors are equally intense.

Be Creative

"What we have to learn to do, we learn by doing."
—Aristotle

The best instruction is only a beginning point. While instruction points you in the right direction, it cannot make you a good artist. Experience is truly a better teacher than the instruction. Skill comes from doing the thing and the discoveries that are made along the way. In knowing this you can be bold in the things you try. There is no one right way to handle a medium like pastel. The experience of trying many different approaches is how you become proficient. As Aristotle says, "...we learn by doing."

TRY IT: Pack up your pastels, and take a trip outdoors. Find something that catches your interest and draw it. Try any new ways of handling the medium of pastel that you think of. Often a new scene will evoke a new way of using the materials as you try to describe what you see with those materials.

OBJECTIVE: to encourage a sense of discovery in using the new medium of pastels, while gaining inspiration from new surroundings.

Look at Secondary Colors in Art

In this work by Franz Marc, secondary colors of green and orange are used with the primary color blue. By limiting the colors he chose to work with, Marc simplified the work. It is pleasing to look at because of the way the orange deer and path wind through the picture space. Black is used to give solidity to areas of the work. This helps to make the objects seem grounded as if they are standing in a real space. White is used to highlight areas. This makes the neck of the deer and the cloud formations stand out from the background. Pastel work lends itself to the kind of simple color choices found in this work of art.

Franz Marc, *Red Deers II*, 1912. Photo Credit: Dover Publications Inc., NY.

The artist chose to use only three colors from the secondary and primary color choices available. He lightens the blue color, making the green and orange stand out.

The Artist

Franz Marc (1880-1916) German Expressionist Painter

Franz Marc was born in Munich, the capital of Bavaria, Germany. His father was a painter of landscapes. In 1911, Marc founded the *Der Blaue Reiter* journal. The Blue Rider group was the first Modern art group in Germany. Marc displayed many works of brightly colored animals in unnaturally colored settings. Marc gave emotional meanings to the colors used in his work. Blue was used for masculinity and spirituality, while yellow was used for joy. Once the National Socialists took power under Hitler, they suppressed the new movement. In 1936 and 1937, the Nazis condemned Marc as a degenerate artist, along with many of his friends. They ordered that 130 of his works be taken from exhibits in German museums. Mar was called to serve under the German military and died in combat.

The Culture

SOCIALIST POLICIES ON ART

Under Nazi occupation, German artists experimenting with bright colors and bold applications of color were labeled degenerate. This label had drastic consequences, which included dismissal from teaching positions, being forbidden to exhibit or to sell their art, and in some cases being forbidden to produce art entirely. In many ways Expressionist art came from the existentialist philosophies being discussed at the time, but the vulgarity of the art was largely due to the actions of the Socialist Party. Their agenda included war, impoverishment, and extermination of people types and people groups. Reactions against these atrocities became a part of the Expressionist's subject matter.

The Challenge

When using pastels, colors are layered over others. They are not mixed as when using paints. Layer colors in this challenge. Draw an object that uses a primary color and secondary colors that sit next to it on the color wheel. For example, you might choose a red apple using secondary colors of orange for the highlights and purple for shading. You might draw a yellow pear using green, a secondary color, for shading.

After applying a few layers of color to the paper, you may find that you cannot lay down another color in that area because the paper is full of powdered pigment. You can revive your drawing by spraying it with hairspray and then letting it dry. The paper will curl when wet, but uncurls once it dries. The hairspray renews a textured surface so that more pastel can be applied. Apply a final coat of fixative (hairspray) to the paper when finished.

HOW TO LAYER PASTELS

It is important to understand how colors mix so that when you layer one color over another, you are not surprised by the results. You can combine two colors to come up with a third color when you know which colors to use. Place one primary color over another, as shown, to make a secondary color. Some colors are purer than others are, so try to use the brightest colors in your set. Below you can see what colors to layer to get orange, green, and violet. You can also use those colors provided in your set, but at times, you'll want to layer.

Colored paper is a favorite choice for pastel artists. You can see in the example below that colors look even more intense (bright) when drawn on colored paper. You will use both white and colors throughout this book.

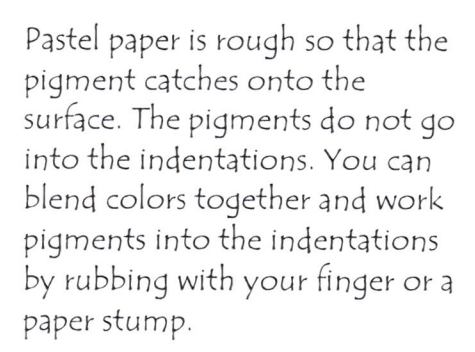

Pastel paper is rough so that the pigment catches onto the surface. The pigments do not go into the indentations. You can blend colors together and work pigments into the indentations by rubbing with your finger or a paper stump.

Once you have a smooth, blended surface, you can go back over areas with other colors. Highlights can be added using white pastel.

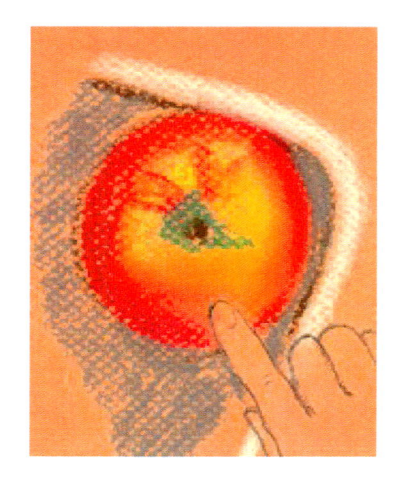
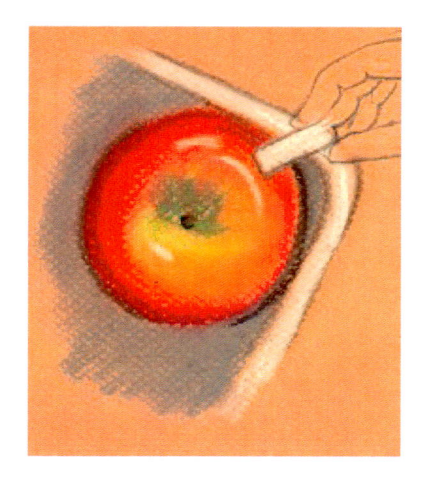

Try New Techniques

Choose some bright fruit or vegetables and draw them from a high viewpoint on colored paper. Use the method of blending with your finger or a paper stump as shown.

The Project

Draw a picture in pastel using a photograph as a reference. Choose a photograph that uses primary and secondary colors. Outdoor scenes or pictures of birds are usually colorful. When using a photograph, it is best to place it as close to the drawing paper as possible. Secure it to a drawing board next to the drawing paper as shown. This allows quick eye movements from photo to drawing, resulting in a more accurate drawing. When finished, apply fixative (hairspray) to the drawing. If you do not have a drawing board, you can work on a flat table in much the same way.

Materials

- hard pastels
- kneaded eraser
- white pastel paper
- chamois, cotton ball, or paper stump
- drawing board
- aerosol hairspray

Student Gallery

Student work by J. C. uses purple and orange in the sky. Purple is reflected in the water too. Green is also used.

References

Find a photograph in a magazine that shows a subject you are interested in. Good photographs are found in nature or popular magazines. Your subject may be:

- machines
- birds
- aircraft
- boats
- wild animals
- forest creatures
- flower arrangements
- buildings

LOOK BACK! Did you use primary or secondary colors in the drawing? Among those learned so far, which techniques for drawing in pastel did you use in this drawing?

UNIT 3
monochrome

Tinting and shading refer to a color's value. If a whole painting uses only one color, but shows different tints and shades of that color, it is based on a monochromatic color scheme.

To **tint** is to make any hue found on the color wheel **lighter.**

To **shade** is to make any hue found on the color wheel **darker.**

Be Creative

"Creativity is inventing, experimenting, growing, taking risks, breaking rules, making mistakes, and having fun." –Mary Lou Cook

The quote above by Mary Lou Cook, an author and co-author of books on artistry and creativity, defines creativity as not one thing, but something that has many components. Let's take time to think about each one and what it means to an artist. Inventing involves imagination and results in coming up with new ideas. The symbolists that you will study in this unit were strongly in favor of using imagination. Experimenting involves trying those ideas out and doing things that may or may not work, which includes taking risks and making mistakes. Growing is a gradual process that includes all those things as a part of moving forward into new areas, with the experiences of the past to support your knowledge and progression. Breaking rules may be one of the hardest ideas to include in creativity, but in light of the recent past century, breaking the old rules was the thing that got artists attention from the public. In the past artists like the Symbolists needed to break strict rules that defined what art should and should not look like. Today so many rules have been broken that we all feel a desire to find and use some rules again. Rules like how to use tinting and shading in a work of art or how the color wheel works can help our art look better. Finally, fun just is a component of creativity because we are allowed to show something of ourselves in a process in which we have control.

TRY IT: Explore creativity. What is the one thing you would love to draw, but has not yet fit one of the assignments in this book? That is the drawing you should try today using the components of creativity. Make the drawing with pastels, using the knowledge you've gained so far.

OBJECTIVE: to explore an idea or subject matter that sounds interesting, involving the creative components of inventing, experimenting, taking risks, and having fun.

Look at Monochrome in Art

Mono means one. Monochrome is one color. A monochromatic color scheme uses mostly one color. It can be just as interesting as a painting done with a full range of colors when it contains sharp contrasts in value. Value, the lightness or darkness of a color, is a very powerful element. This work is based on the color blue. It is made lighter with white in the sheep and the woman. The painting reaches its darkest value at the top of the ridge. By placing the woman's head and shirt, (both light) against the dark ridge in the background, the figure stands out.

Alphonse Osbert (1857-1939) *Vision* 1892. Photo Credit : Dover Publications Inc.

Dark values

Middle values

Light values

The figure changes gradually from light to dark. The background directly behind her changes from a dark ridge to light grasses, creating contrast.

The Artist

Alphonse Osbert (1857-1939)
French Symbolist Painter

Professors at the Ecole des Beaux Arts in the late 1800's were teaching students to paint in the traditional ways painting had been practiced for centuries. They saw nature in dark browns and subdued colors. They painted with smooth brush strokes, sometimes making little wispy strokes for leaves or branches. They went outdoors to make small, yet detailed paintings called studies, and then retreated to studios to make the finished painting. Alphonse Osbert grew tired of the method. In his search for something new he studied the pointillism method that artists, Seurat and Signac, were developing. He eventually found that he wanted to explore the area of ideas in his works, rather than search for new techniques of applying the paint to the canvas. He left the depiction of real-world subject matter and developed a poetic, imaginary style. His figures appear in misty or mysterious landscapes. Light often comes from the sun or moon, which baths the figures and gives the sense that one is in a dream.

The Culture

THE SYMBOLIST PAINTER

Symbolism was developed in the late 1800's in France as a way to explore the imagination and those things that are not clearly seen in the physical world we live in. It was explored through literature, poetry, and art. In art, the focus was especially strong on making images that illustrated the great literature of the past. Greek figures, such as Ulysses who was tormented by the Sirens and Icarus who flew too close to the sun, are found in their paintings as well as characters like Merlin from King Author's legends. Influential authors such as William Shakespeare inspired artists to explore images that included fairies and wood nymphs. Symbolists wrote manifestoes to map out their ideas. They attracted many different ideas. All ideas were an attempt to bring spirituality back into their lives. The hard science and the atheistic beliefs that had led to decadent behavior and tortured artistic images of the expressionists were not for everyone. The paintings are technically very realistic. The figures are drawn sharply and precisely. Trees and landscapes are rendered with accurate and careful detail. The realistic nature of the images attracted a large audience, especially those not attracted to the decadent expressionistic art that was developing at the same time.

The Challenge

Draw a monochromatic picture in pastel. Use only one color and its variations (sky blue, royal blue, dark blue, etc.), plus white to tint and black to shade. Look for values in the subject. Draw values as accurately as possible, but do not be concerned with details. Apply fixative (hairspray) to the drawing when finished.

HOW TO MAKE A DRY WASH

A wash usually refers to pigment in water that is applied to the paper in a smooth even layer. A dry wash uses no water, but creates a similar effect. **1.** To make a dry wash, use the side of your pastels, making wide strokes in layers covering the entire paper. Using a cotton ball, rub the dry pigment into the paper, in a small circular motion. Some of the pigment will fall off and you can dump the extra pigment into a trashcan. You can also use a shammy cloth for rubbing instead of the cotton ball.

1.

2.

2. Draw figures over the smooth background. Blend, with a blending stump, in areas that are too small to blend with a cotton ball or chamois. Use the blending stump by rubbing the flat side or the tip back and forth to blend colors.

The finished work is monochrome – blue on orange paper. The dry wash makes a soft background for the two figures.

Try New Techniques

Work from a family photograph, using it as a reference. Use a monochrome color scheme. Black and white can be used with the color you choose. Choose a colored paper that is very different from the color chosen for the picture.

The Project

Draw a picture using subjects in imaginative ways like the Symbolists. The subject matter can deal with any type of spiritual or imagined imagery. Pastel is a fun medium to use for imagined images because it is easy to erase the image by wiping it out with a chamois or cotton ball and starting again. The layers build up. This work does not need to be entirely monochromatic, however work with a simple group of colors.

Student Gallery

This work is by J. C. and shows a face in the sky. This work is imagined, yet based on a real face. A mountain range is shown on the lower portion of the picture.

Materials

- hard pastels
- kneaded eraser
- cotton ball
- chamois
- pastel paper
- aerosol hairspray

References

You can use photographs for references or work directly from your imagination. In this way, imagery is used but not copied directly. Settings for your symbolist picture might be:

- sky
- water
- nightfall
- sunrise
- forest
- desert
- cliff and ocean

LOOK BACK! Did you use imagination to make a picture? How are the realistic subjects in the picture used in unrealistic ways?

The Elements Combined- Color and Form

1.

2.

Choose a photograph to work from. Then follow the steps shown. The photograph for this pastel drawing was taken from a low viewpoint to get a more exciting angle. 1. Secure the paper to the table top or drawing board surface with tape on the corners. Using light pastel on colored paper, begin to outline the object in the photograph using the correct colors. Do not make black outlines because these will smear. Draw and redraw over lines until you like the placement. Begin to fill in shapes with color.

2. Use a blending stump to smooth over areas. This pushes the color into the recesses of the paper and by filling them up, makes the color look darker. As colors are blended, the form of the object appears. Here, black is gently rubbed with a paper stump to smooth out the area. Continue to work on the entire picture in this way, always redrawing when necessary.

3.

3. Form is created when highlights are added. Here yellow, orange, and white are used for the red car. In the final stages, the sides of light blue and dark blue pastels were rubbed across the paper to create a rough background. This surface contrasts with the smooth form of the car.

UNIT 4
complementary pairs

Complementary pairs are those pairs opposite each other on the color wheel. People have noticed that these pairs, when put side by side seem especially vibrant. One can use a **complementary color scheme** in a painting by using one of the pairs below.

Be Creative

"Originality exists in every individual because each of us differs from the other."
–Jean Guitton

Some occasions happen rarely and the artist needs to be ready when opportunity shows itself. One morning after a very heavy rain, I noticed mushrooms in the yard. Exploring near the woods, I discovered plant life in colors like I'd never seen them before. Bright red fungi sprouted from deep, warm blacks of wet, rotting wood. Vibrant greens lay against woods made brilliant red by the soaking. I drew throughout the day, knowing that it would all be gone tomorrow.

Take advantage of an opportune moment. Part of originality comes from what you notice in the world, and that will be different from what others notice.

TRY IT: Look for activity around your home. The evening meal may be one of those times when family members sit, talk, gesture, and laugh. Prepare your art tools and draw a sketch of the scene as it happens. Later develop it using color. Your work will be original because the subject is chosen and interpreted by you.

OBJECTIVE: to begin to think like an artist by observing and taking advantage of opportunities to draw scenes of daily life.

Look at Complementary Pairs

A complementary color scheme consists of one primary color and the secondary color opposite it on the color wheel. If you look at a color wheel, you'll notice that red and green, yellow and violet, and blue and orange are the three complementary pairs. These hues, when placed side by side seem to vibrate, or intensify each other. In this work by Redon, the most prominent colors are red in the foreground and green in the background. Where are blue and orange found together? Is yellow and violet found in the picture?

In the section of this picture below, you can more easily see how the pastel is applied to the neutral brown paper.

Odilon Redon (1840-1916) *Vase au Guerrier Japonais, Photo* Credit: Dover Publications Inc., NY.

Dabs of green pastel over brown paper.

Find lines on top of solidly colored areas.

White on brown paper and rubbed for a smooth surface, then outlined in blue.

The Artist

Odilon Redon (1840-1916)
French Symbolist Painter

Redon used symbolic imagery in much of his art. He pulled subject matter from both the things he saw in life and the things he saw in dreams. He was part of a group called the Symbolists. While the Impressionists were looking for a more direct way to show what nature looked like, the Symbolists did not desire to show a view of the natural world. They wanted to show a view of things they could not see, such as dreams and what they could imagine. Redon used brilliant hues and worked in pastels on colored paper as well as lithography, charcoal, and oil paints.

The Culture

Symbolism was a reaction against realism as it had developed in European culture since the time of the Renaissance. The idea of making something look as real as possible was fresh and new in the 14th and 15th centuries, but the discoveries that were made at that time had been reworked in the centuries that followed and became mere rules with no inspiration. The Symbolist movement invited spirituality and the use of imagination. They looked at their dreams for inspiration. Men pursued these outlets without a spiritual belief in God. The artworks are often described as dark. They painted the fears of humankind and often drew inspiration from literary works of authors like Edgar Allan Poe. Symbolism was a philosophy or set of ideals which captured the imaginations of late 19th century artists. It was distinctly separate from Impressionism in ideals, but happened at the same period.

The Challenge

Look for complimentary pairs in or around your home. You may find a red object, like a brick building, against a green landscape. Draw a sketch in pastel from your observations. Apply fixative (hairspray) to the drawing when finished. Here red and green complimentary colors are used with black and white on brown wrapping paper.

  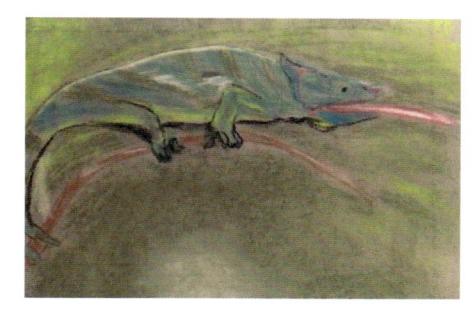

These student works from left to right are by Daniel, Uriah, and Eric. All were done on brown wrapping paper.

HOW TO DRAW ON A DARK BACKGROUND

Achieve a dramatic look using dark pastel paper or black construction paper. The dark background not only makes the complementary colors of red and green stand out, but also shows off white and other light colors that are usually unnoticed when working on white paper.

To begin, draw lines in color. Layer colors over each other, while allowing the black to show through in places.

These colors were used in the drawing below.

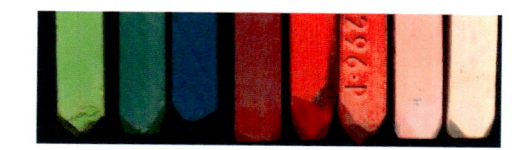

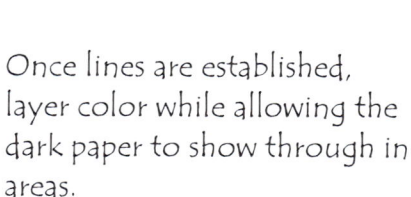

Draw lines describing each object in the colors of that object. By doing this you can get a better idea of how the composition will look. Changes in lines, colors, or arrangement can be made easier at this stage in the drawing.

Once lines are established, layer color while allowing the dark paper to show through in areas.

The completed work shows large areas of black paper. Black plays a major part in the picture while creating intensity.

NOTE: Care should be taken to place colors side by side so that they intensify one another. If mixed or blended with your finger, the color will have the opposite effect, becoming dull.

Try New Techniques

Set up a still life arrangement and draw on dark pastel paper. Use the technique of drawing the first lines in the colors that you see on those objects, instead of drawing them all in the same color. When finished, spray a light mist of hairspray over the drawing.

The Project

Draw a still life on dark paper. Set up a still life using an object or objects found in the home. Use objects with different shapes or textures for added interest. Overlap some or all of the objects so that they connect. Arrange the objects until you have a pleasing set up. Apply fixative (hairspray) to the drawing when finished.

Student Gallery

Student work by Caleb Garrison uses complementary colors side by side in the vegetables. Red and green are also picked up in the pot. While we think about a carrot being orange, this orange is very much within the red hue, creating intensity when placed beside the green cucumber.

Materials

- pastels
- kneaded eraser
- dark pastel paper or construction paper
- aerosol hairspray

References

Set up a still life using colorful objects from around the home. You might look in the following places:

- kitchen or pantry for fruit and vegetables
- playroom for colorful toys
- garage for tools with colorful handles
- library for colorful books and figurines
- family room for trophies or other objects of family interest

LOOK BACK! Did you set up a still life and work directly from it? Did you use color lines to draw the still life?

UNIT 5
neutrals

When complimentary pairs are mixed, they become less intense and make neutral colors. Neutral colors are described as brown or gray. Neutral colors vary when different complementary pairs are mixed.

Be Creative

"The universe is God's work of art. God's creation established the foundational necessities–the physical, aesthetic, and human realities–that make subsequent art possible."

–Gene Edward Veith, Jr., Author

One must actively seek inspiration. Inspiration does not seek people out nor does it tend to appear magically when we need it. It is tough to get inspired while sitting in a room that is familiar to you. So where do you go for inspiration? Get closer to nature, the work of a creative hand. The Psalmist states, "The heavens declare the glory of God: and the firmament (earth) shows His handiwork." (Ps. 19:1, the New King James Version). Step outdoors; look, observe natural things.

TRY IT: Go outdoors and away from your house if possible. Look up at the sky. Look down at the ground. Look to distant scenes. Find inspiration.

OBJECTIVE: to encourage active participation in finding meaningful, inspiring subjects for art.

CREATIVE CORY

Cory had to use your vehicle for the still life, dear. He says he saw it all in a moment of inspiration.

Look at Neutral Colors in Art

We often name neutral colors brown or gray. All colors can be lowered in intensity until they become brown or gray. They have different qualities depending on which colors are used in the mix. In this pastel work by Degas, we see different neutral colors. The wall has a light yellow hue. The hat on top of the stand is also a yellow-neutral color. It is less intense than the wall. The stand and object in the woman's hands is a reddish-brown. The lady's dress is a gray neutral color. Gray is also seen in other parts of the picture. The picture is much more interesting because there are so many variations in brown.

Neutral color with emphasis on yellow.

Neutral color with emphasis on red.

Grays are neutral too. Some grays are more blue, some more yellow, and some more red. This gray has an emphasis on red.

Edgar Degas, *At the Milliners*, c.1905–10 Pastel on tracing paper. Photo Credit: Dover Publications Inc., NY.

29

The Artist

Edgar Degas (1834–1917)
French Impressionist Painter

Early in his career, Edgar Degas wanted to be a history painter. He was well trained within the traditional Academy style. In his 30's he changed course. He was part of the Impressionist movement and was influenced greatly by their ideas; however, he did not want to be called an Impressionist. He preferred to think of himself as a realistic painter. His subject matter became more modern as he sought out subjects in ballet studios, at the horse track, and in workplaces like the hat shop in the picture, *At the Milliners*. He was greatly influenced by the new invention of photography and was noted for composing his paintings like a snapshot. He cut off figures, like the figure on the right in the work you just looked at, painting them at the edge of the canvas or paper. Degas worked in pastels, perhaps more often than any other Impressionist painter, except for Cassatt, who greatly admired the work of Degas. Pastels could be applied to the paper quickly and could be carried on location easily.

The Culture

Even though Edgar Degas was well educated at the art academy and knew all the rules involved with painting, his work was at odds with the academic standards when he pushed figures to the edges of a painting or part way out of it. In an academic work, the figures would be placed well within the edges of the picture. By doing this, the artist showed a complete picture or idea. Degas' figures, leaning out of the edges, suggest that the world goes on beyond this single idea or format. It suggests a world that the artist has only hinted at. The Chinese created similar worlds in their hand held scroll paintings. A long strip of silk or paper was rolled into a scroll and a continuous landscape was painted onto the scroll. The viewer only saw a piece at a time as he unrolled one end while rolling the other up. One view led into the next, suggesting a world beyond the one we see. Degas would not have been aware of Chinese scrolls. It was the new invention of photography that influenced his technique. He saw the way snapshots caught a moment with people or animals going into and out of the picture. The result of Degas' work and of the Chinese scroll was that art captured a segment of time and space while suggesting that there was more to be seen.

The Challenge

Make a chart of neutral colors to use for future reference. Find at least ten combinations and variations of neutral colors using all the colors in your pastel set. Label each combination with the hues that were used in the mixture. When finished, apply fixative (hairspray) to the chart. Keep the chart for future reference.

HOW TO DRAW SKIN COLORS

One does not need many colors to make a satisfying portrait when using a colored background. The pastels at the right of the two pictures show which colors were used. Select the flesh tones from your pastels. Conte crayons often come in flesh tones and are very similar to hard pastels.

A medium-dark paper is chosen as a background for the dark skin of the man. The face is not completely filled in but the paper shows in some areas. The entire portrait uses only neutral colors.

Light paper is chosen as a background for the light skin of the girl. The blue colors seen in shaded areas of the skin reflect the colors around the face. These colors are not found within the skin itself. These shaded areas tie in with the blue shirt and give unity to the portrait.

Try New Techniques

Draw a portrait of a person using color paper and pastels. Work from a photograph that shows the form of the face. Look for both highlights and shaded areas. Apply fixative (hairspray) to the finished work.

The Project

Draw a self-portrait from your image as seen in a mirror. Use neutral colors.

To be successful with pastels it is helpful to look at the work of those who used pastels in the past. Mary Cassatt and Edgar Degas were especially skilled in its use and are perhaps our best instructors in this medium. Look for the following practices in their work:

- They worked large. Creating details within a small area is difficult when one applies color with a stick.
- They worked on color backgrounds. It is not unusual to begin with a color background in other media but it is of special benefit when working with pastels. The light colored pastels are opaque when placed over a dark background, creating an immediate contrast of light and dark.
- They worked in loose strokes, placing color beside color. This is especially suited to pastels because they are difficult to blend.

This work shows how pastels can be applied loosely, while layering one color over another.

Materials

- Flesh tone pastels
- kneaded eraser
- cotton ball
- chamois
- pastel paper
- aerosol hairspray
- mirror

References

Set up a mirror and observe your face and shoulders in it. Sit your drawing materials in front of you as you face the mirror.

NOTE: Self-portrait mirrors are available for art students. These plastic mirrors stand up, making it easy to see a reflection while working from a table.

Student Gallery

Student work by Geoffrey Lohr uses quick strokes in a layered effect.

LOOK BACK! Did you use light and dark colors to contrast with the neutral background of the color paper?

The Elements Combined– Shapes and Values

Take a photograph and work from it. Follow these steps using pastels on white paper.

1. Draw the shapes with a neutral color. Wipe out with lines with a chamois so that they show faintly. Then redraw, making corrections as needed.

2. Fill in spaces with color and wipe with a chamois to spread color evenly.

3. Add a few skin colors on top.

4. Use a paper stump to blend and spread color. The stump works the pigment into the paper. The effect of filling in the white spaces of the paper is that the colors look darker. Place dark values over lighter ones.

5. Color is used sparingly. Only purple is added for the shirt. The artist pays attention to the values. 6. The final work shows that the dark value of the countertop was added to frame the child and the bowl, making them stand out.

UNIT 6
warm
ANALOGOUS COLORS

Analogous colors are hues that sit beside each other on the color wheel.

When analogous colors are mixed, they do not loose intensity or brightness.

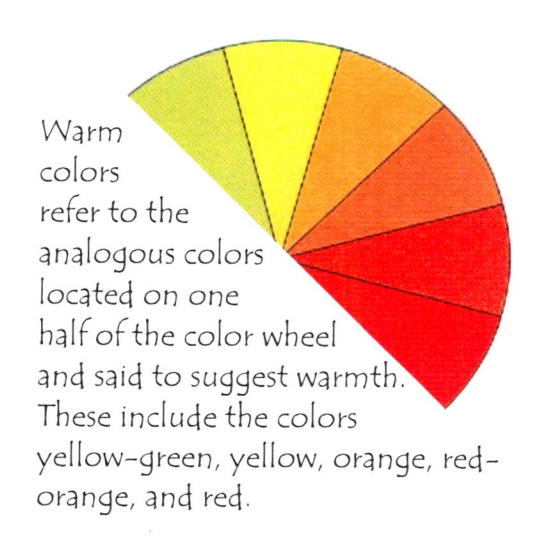

Warm colors refer to the analogous colors located on one half of the color wheel and said to suggest warmth. These include the colors yellow-green, yellow, orange, red-orange, and red.

Be Creative

Make a list of warm places such as Phoenix, Arizona in the American southwest, pavement in summer, or a summer garden. List at least five places. Find information about the habitat of one of these areas. What types of wildlife live there? What types of plant life thrive there? Is the landscape made of sand dunes, mountains, bare rock, gravel, pavement, or steel? What is the temperature during the day? Observe the place in real life or through pictures. Keep the list of your observations in a portfolio as a reference for future drawings and paintings.

TRY IT: Choose one hot place. Imagine a scene of the place you choose. Draw the scene using warm colors. When finished, fix the drawing with hairspray.

OBJECTIVE: to consider what types of situations or places in which one might see warm colors and to use imagination as a tool for ideas.

CREATIVE CORY

Cory said he needed to add substance to his imagination by getting a look at the real thing.

Look at Warm Colors in Art

Color can stir emotion or cause certain feelings to occur. Once aware of the emotional aspects of color, the artist can use color to help create the feel he or she wants in the painting. Colors are said to be warm or cool. Red, orange, and yellow have the power to suggest warmth. In this picture, the ripening fields of grain have become yellow. The Samurai on Horseback race on warm colored roads under a warm summer sky.

Hokusai. *Samurai on Horseback*, 1826. Photo Credit: Dover Publications Inc.

Yellow and yellow-green in the areas shown at the right give warm tones to this picture.

The Artist

Katsushika Hokusai, (1760-1849) JAPANESE UKIYO-E PAINTER

Hokusai made numerous Japanese prints and is one of the best-known Japanese artists of all time. His landscapes appeal to Western culture because the West influenced them. The Japanese consumer preferred samurai and actors portraits. Hokusai was a bit of a rebel. He liked to play with new ideas. He began painting landscapes. This very non-traditional full landscape includes a strange mixture of Samurai equestrians and common laborers. We can see nature's influence on Hokusai when in the postscript to "One Hundred Views of Mount Fuji", Hokusai writes, "From around the age of six, I had the habit of sketching from life. I became an artist, and from fifty on began producing works that won some reputation, but nothing I did before the age of seventy was worthy of attention. At seventy-three, I began to grasp the structures of birds and beasts, insects and fish, and of the way plants grow. If I go on trying, I will surely understand them still better by the time I am eighty-six, so that by ninety I will have penetrated to their essential nature. At one hundred, I may well have a positively divine understanding of them, while at one hundred and thirty, forty, or more I will have reached the stage where every dot and every stroke I paint will be alive." Although Hokusai did not live to one hundred and forty, the works he created do have life in every stroke, just as he was hoping to accomplish.

The Culture

EUROPE'S INFLUENCE ON JAPAN AND JAPAN'S INFLUENCE ON EUROPE

The idea of landscape painting came to Japan from the West. The works of Dutch painters, who had made landscape painting popular from 1600- 1700's in Holland, were produced as cheap illustrations. Dutch merchants smuggled goods into Japan, wrapped in artists etchings, used as throwaway wrappers. Hokusai and other artists learned about perspective through these discarded works and transformed Dutch landscape painting into something that was Japanese. Later, as these Japanese prints were so well received and created in large numbers, they were discarded and used as packing material for imports going from Japan to Europe. The Impressionists saw these works and were greatly influenced by the work of Hokusai. They picked up his simplicity of form and pattern. Therefore, European art was mixed into Japanese and then sent back to Europe where Japanese art mixed into European art. After the 1800's the art of most cultures would not be isolated, but would influence and be influenced by cultures from all around the world.

The Challenge

Use pencil or pastels. Draw a quick sketch of a scene that is taking place in your home. It may include family members or pets. Is someone working? Draw that. Is someone playing? Draw that.

HOW TO USE A WARM COLOR SCHEME

Warm color papers are available in large sheets at art supply stores.

A friendly mood is created using warm colors on warm color paper. These colors are used in the drawing below.

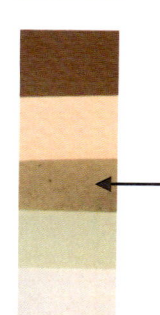

Warm, neutral colors are also available. The center color is brown shipping paper. It holds the pastel well, is cheap, and is readily available.

Warm colors set the mood as friendly and inviting.

Try New Techniques

Arrange both pastels and color paper into groups of warm colors and colors that do not seem warm. Remember that neutral colors like brown or gray can be warm or cool. To find out, decide if they lean more to a yellow hue or to a blue hue. If they seem more yellow, then they are warm. Arrange and draw a group of objects that are warm in hue. When finished, apply fixative to the paper using a light mist of hairspray.

The Project

Draw a picture in pastels using a warm color scheme. Consider the color of the paper. It should add to the warm feel of the drawing. When finished, apply fixative (hairspray) to the picture in a light mist.

Materials

- warm color pastels
- kneaded eraser
- warm color paper
- aerosol hairspray
- cotton ball
- chamois
- blending stump

Student Gallery

Student work by Caleb Garrison uses yellows and warm grays.

References

Find objects that are warm in color. Obviously anything that is red, yellow, or orange falls into that category. Think about warm neutral colors too. Gray can be warm. Brown can be warm. Look in:

- kitchen cabinets
- on shelves throughout the house
- in a relative's kitchen cabinets
- on a relative's shelves

Some homes are filled with more objects than yours might be. Do ask friends and relatives if you can borrow objects to draw.

LOOK BACK! Does your picture suggest warmth? What kind of effect do the colors in your picture have on the viewer? Does it make them feel a certain way?

UNIT 7 COOL
ANALOGOUS COLORS

Analogous colors are hues that sit beside each other on the color wheel.

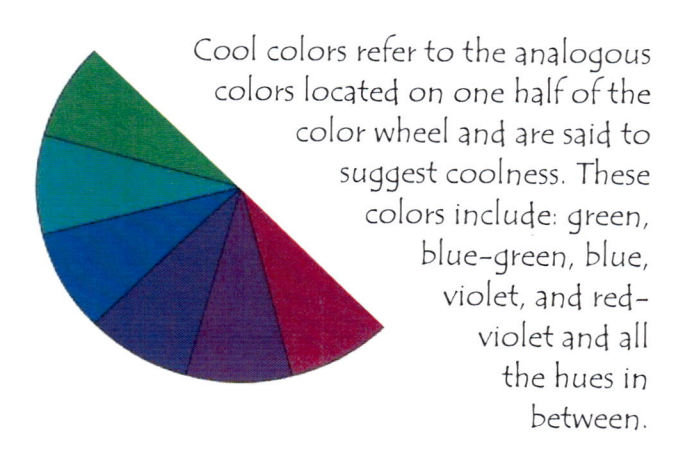

Cool colors refer to the analogous colors located on one half of the color wheel and are said to suggest coolness. These colors include: green, blue-green, blue, violet, and red-violet and all the hues in between.

Be Creative

The light of the sun, or the absence of it, affects the colors of objects seen outdoors. The absence of sunshine usually has a cooling effect. Think about times when you have noticed cool colors outdoors. Make a list of at least five different weather situations that are accompanied by cool colors such as a rainstorm, snowstorm, or fog.

TRY IT: Choose one weather situation and imagine the scene. Place characters or subjects in it if you like. Draw the scene using a cool color scheme. When finished, apply fixative (hairspray) to the picture. Spray the picture with a light mist, holding the hairspray about twelve inches from the drawing.

Keep the list created above as a reference for future paintings and drawings.

OBJECTIVE: to consider what types of weather situations suggest coolness and to use imagination as a tool for ideas.

CREATIVE CORY

CORY GOES TO EXTREMES IN THE COOL WEATHER ASSIGNMENT.

Look at Cool Colors in Art

Green, blue, and violet are referred to as cool colors. Look at the way Wassily Kandinsky uses blue in the shadows and sky. Blue is also used on the shaded side of the home on the right. A snow scene, as in his painting of this churchyard in Kochel Russia, is a perfect place to find cool colors. The contrast of the warm yellow buildings helps the blue areas to appear cooler.

Wassily Kandinsky, *Church Yard and Vicarage in Kochel,* 1909. Photo Credit: Dover Publications, Inc., NY.

The deep blue in the snowy shadows and sky place this painting on the cool side of the color wheel.

The Artist

Wassily Kandinsky (1866-1944)
Russian Expressionist Painter

Kandinsky began his career by experimenting with bright colors and color combinations in realistic scenes like this landscape. His work gradually changed so that the bright colors were used in very abstract ways. Kandinsky provided a theory for abstract art that others could understand and build upon.

The Challenge

Since pastels are powdered pigments, they can be brushed with water to create a painting medium. Choose a subject you like and follow the directions below for creating a pastel painting. If you do not have a brush available, use the blending stump (dry) for a similar effect.

The Culture

RUSSIA

In a very general sense, the history of Russian art followed the trends of painting that had developed within other European nations. Russian artists broke from this trend to create innovative art in the first few decades of the 20th century. In 1919, avant-garde artist, Kandinsky helped to organize twenty-two new museums across the Soviet Union. The Russian Revolution of 1917 soon turned from a people's movement, which allowed this great burst of creative output, to a dictatorship. The new conservative direction of socialist realism put an end to all expressive and creative ideas in art. Socialist realism describes art that serves only to support the ideals set forth by the current dictator. It was not art created by free citizens or for the citizens.

On a sheet of sturdy paper, draw the outline lightly with pastels. Color in the spaces.

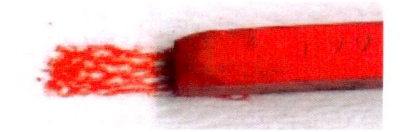

Go over the colored areas with a wet brush. The color becomes more intense as pigment fills in the white spaces.

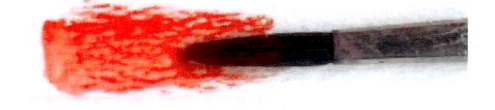

HOW TO USE A COOL COLOR SCHEME

These bright, cool colors are available in large sheets.

These neutral, cool colors are also available in large sheets.

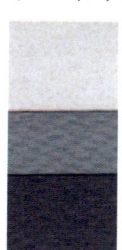

These cool colors were used in the work below.

In the drawing below, various blue tints are used on bright blue paper to make a cool landscape. Cool colors seem to go back in space, while warm colors seem to pull forward. The two steps below show how easy it is to manipulate pastels, changing lines, and adding objects.

1. Blue paper is used as a background color. Areas of color are laid down directly in the first step with no need to outline the subjects.

2. Colors are blended with a cotton swab or finger. Boulders are added, the tree expanded, and the shoreline changed to add more interest to the drawing. White highlights are added to the surface of water and tree. Dark colors are added to the boulders and shoreline for contrast.

Try New Techniques

Look for cool colors in small objects found outdoors. Draw a pile of rocks, group of plants, a front yard display, or any group of objects where you can observe and draw with cool colors.

The Project

Draw a landscape using a cool color scheme. Work directly on the paper as shown on the previous page. Draw in large areas of color. Change and manipulate the drawing as needed, until you have interest and contrast. Find something within the scene that is in the warm color range to contrast with the cool colors. When finished, fix the pastel to the page with hairspray.

Student Gallery

Student work, left, by Caleb Garrison uses cool greens and blues. The warm reddish-brown colors contrast with the cool colors around them.

Materials

- cool color pastels
- kneaded eraser
- cool color paper
- chamois
- aerosol hairspray

References

Look for cool landscapes or scenes around your area. If you cannot find a cool scene, look for one in a photograph. Cool color scenes may appear in these conditions:

- evening just after sunset
- winter
- where snow is a part of the scene
- water and sky
- in shadows

LOOK BACK! Did you find a landscape with a cool color scheme? Did you use cool colors? Did you choose to use some warm colors to contrast with the cool ones?

UNIT 8
color Application

How the marks are applied to, the paper has an effect on the mood of the picture.

The very rapid strokes in the drawing on the left create the impression of a light breezy day with shifting clouds. When orange hues and soft strokes are applied to the same scene, at right, the mood is calmer.

Be Creative

Artists often paint the same subject because it holds great interest for them. One such artist was Claude Monet. He said, "I have painted the Seine (a river) all my life, at all hours of the day, and in every season…I have never been bored with it: to me it is always different." To make this approach work find a subject you really have interest in. See the subtle differences in that subject and attempt to capture them on paper.

TRY IT: Do a mini-series of an object during sunset, at noon, and night. Claude Monet chose one object and studied it at different times of day and in different weather conditions. Use color to convey effectively the feel of the object at the time of day you are drawing it. A quick sketch might take ten to fifteen minutes from start to finish.

OBJECTIVE: to understand that it is not the subject that makes good art, but how the artist chooses to use that subject.

CREATIVE CORY

I did five drawings of that building today, but I never saw it like this!

Look at Color Application in Art

Colors can be applied to the paper in different ways to create different textures within the artwork. The side of the pastel was used on the purple wall, creating a smooth application that is not filled in. We still see the paper through the area. The end of the pastel is used to create lines or marks in the hair and flower foliage. These marks give the feeling of the texture of those objects. Look at how the artist uses different applications of pastel to make the fan. Can you identify where he has used the side of the pastel, the end, and where he has blended colors?

Jean-Louis Forain, *Woman Smelling Flowers*, 1883.
Photo Credit: Dover Publications Inc.

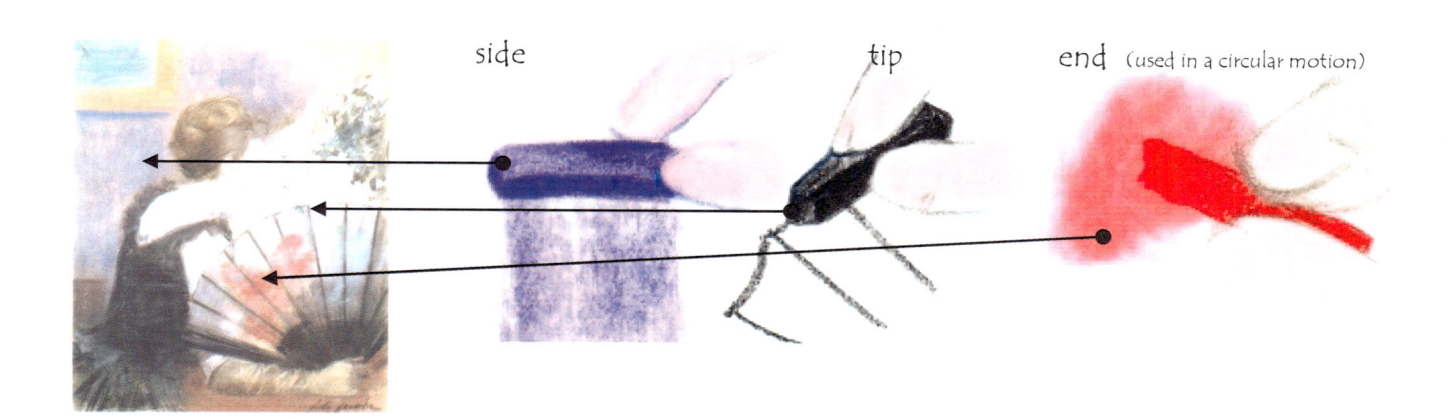

side   tip   end (used in a circular motion)

The Artist

Jean-Louis Forain (1852 - 1931)
French Impressionist Painter and
Printmaker

Forain began his career working as a
caricaturist for several Paris journals and
then went on to study art. He became a
friend of Edgar Degas, another French
Impressionist who specialized in pastel
drawings. Forain participated in four
Impressionist exhibitions between 1879
and 1884. In his later years, Forain
created satires on late 19th and early
20th century French life.

The Culture

THE SATIRE

A satire in graphic art is a comically distorted
drawing or likeness, done with the purpose of
ridiculing its subject. While satires have a long
history, the French developed a special taste for
this type of humor in the nineteenth century
because of their dislike of their leader, Napoléon
Bonaparte I. Passions were high and the satirist
was able to poke fun at the foolish decisions of
the leadership without putting himself in
political danger. Leaders who tried to suppress
Napoleon were also subjected to satirical
criticism and political commentary by cartoon
or caricature. In this way, the caricature was
firmly established.

The Challenge

Select one pastel stick in the middle
value range. Work on white paper.
Draw a favorite subject. Use the pastel
on the side, tip, and end as shown in
the artwork on the previous page.
This work was made by drawing the
figure, then wiping out some lines to
refine and change the figure. The soft
rubbed areas were created in this
process.
Some lines were made thicker while
others are rubbed out or lightened.
These lines were made using the tip
and the end of the pastel stick.

Background and areas of the shirt are
made using the side of the stick.

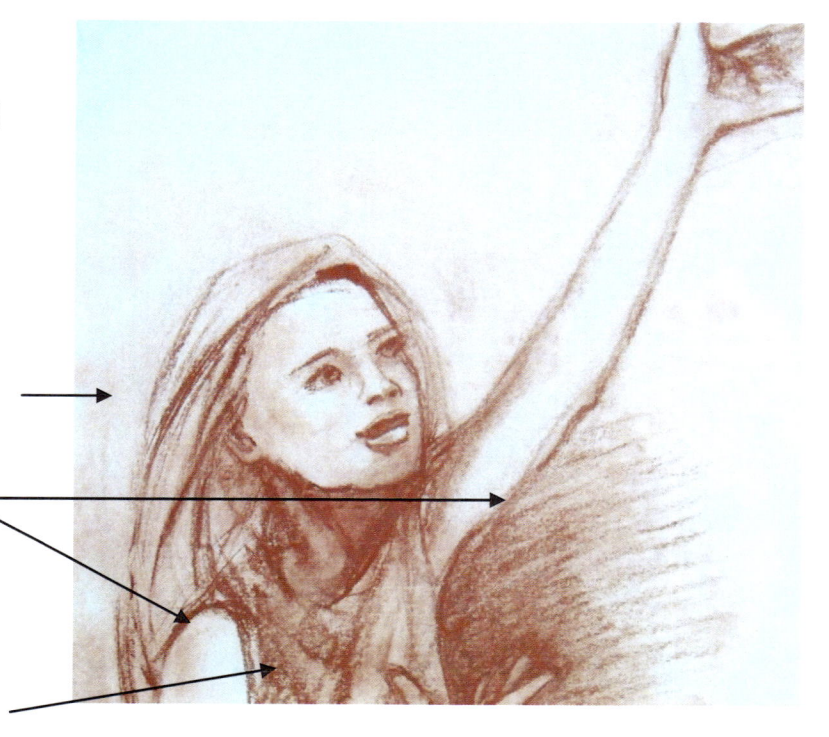

HOW TO APPLY COLOR – DIFFERENT METHODS

Hatching and Crosshatching

This method allows the marks to show. Lines of color are placed side by side over each other. The direction of the strokes conforms to the form of the object. If pastel powder builds up on the paper so that the surface becomes slick and does not allow one color to stay on top of another, recreate a rough surface. To do this, lightly spray the drawing with hairspray in the same manner you apply it to the drawing when it is finished. Let dry. After spraying, draw. Pastels should adhere to the surface again.

Blending

This method erases or softens the marks, but not the color. Color is applied to the paper and rubbed with your finger or a paper stump. Individual strokes are smoothed out. A softer effect is created around the edges of the drawing, blending the table and the background.

Try New Techniques

Draw an object in pastels using one of the methods shown at the right. This drawing was created on brown paper bag. The rough surface and middle range in value found in most brown paper is ideal for pastel work.

47

The Project

Make a picture from a still life that you have set up. Use pastels. Show areas of blending and marks in the picture. You will have both smooth surfaces and roughly drawn surfaces. Seal with hairspray when finished.

Student Gallery

Student work by Caleb Garrison uses the blending technique to smooth the surface of the pots. This contrasts nicely with the rough method used on the surface of the wall. The side of the pastel was used to make the rough surface in the background and on the tabletop.

Materials

- pastels
- kneaded eraser
- stump or cotton ball
- chamois
- white pastel paper
- aerosol hairspray

References

Set up a still life using a variety of objects or observe an object, which has variety in it such as a potted plant. Consider the following:

- Tea set and pot
- Buckets, and tins
- Baking pans
- Flower pots
- Flour and Sugar container set
- Coffee pot
- Tea pot

LOOK BACK! Did you use a rough or smooth method of applying the pastel to the paper? Where in the picture can you see the effects of each?

An artist can bring two major approaches to any piece of art. One approach is to concentrate on rendering the single object. This would include drawing a good outline, shading the form, or studying how the parts of that form fit together. The second approach is to see that form or object as a part of its surroundings. This would include decisions on where to place the form on the page and whether the emphasis of the artwork is on the form or is about something else, such as light or color. Seeing the form as part of its surroundings is a study in composition. Composition is the arrangement of line, texture, shape, form, and value, within the space of the page. Artists arrange and rearrange these elements to find the best or most appealing solutions. Discovering new possibilities for the arrangement of subjects is part of the excitement of making art. New ideas for arrangement are shown in the following units:

- Balance
- Parallel Rhythm
- Converging Rhythm
- Space with Little Depth
- Depth
- Viewpoint, high
- Viewpoint, low
- Emphasis

Composition by student, Mimi Stem, shows rhythm using the color white. Two clouds and two waterfalls catch our attention and create balance within the work as well.

Composition: The arrangement of the elements of art within the space of the picture. It can be accomplished through balance, rhythm, depth, viewpoint and emphasis.

UNIT 9
balance
IN COLOR

Balance is placing the visual elements so that the visual weight feels even across the work as a whole. The element of color should balance. Here is a very simply balanced work. A point, called the vanishing point, marks the center of the picture. The view places the city street in the center so that rows of buildings balance on each side of it. Two trees and a flower garden line up with the street. It is often easy to find balance in manufactured things such as architecture, streets, fields, or gardens.

Be Creative

"The man who makes no mistakes does not usually make anything."

-William Connor Magee, 1868

This statement rings true for artists. It is all right to make mistakes on paper. Artists must learn to look at their work honestly (not critically) and make judgments about it. By evaluating mistakes, artists can improve them and develop their work.

TRY IT: Look over your work from the color assignments in this book. Do they all have balance? Are some better balanced than others are? Check by holding them up to a mirror to see the image backwards. Does one side or part of a picture feel heavy or out of place when viewed this way? You may not be able to correct the problem, but will be more aware when making pictures in the future.

OBJECTIVE: to become more aware of balance in colored works, and to learn to evaluate work for the purpose of improving it.

CREATIVE CORY

Mirror, mirror, on the wall, show mistakes, show them all!

Look at Color Balance in Art

When one looks at a work of art and the eye travels through the space of the painting, the work is balanced. Any of the elements of art can be used to create balance; however, color is one of the strongest elements. In this largely blue and green color scheme, we see bright yellow fruits. On the right is a plate full of pears, while on the left is a lemon. This spot of yellow made by the lemon is powerful enough to pull our eyes away from the pears and towards it. In so doing, the picture balances. The use of two large green objects, the pot and the watermelon, also help our eyes go to the left side of the painting.

Paul Cézanne, *Still Life with a Ginger Jar and Eggplant*, 1893-94.
Photo Credit: Dover Publications Inc.

Green and blue are cool and sit back within the space of this painting. The yellow fruit stands out so the artist must balance this bright color. He does it be placing them on the right and left sides of the center of the painting.

51

The Artist

Paul Cézanne (1839 – 1906)
French Post-Impressionist Painter

Paul Cézanne's work inspired those who would transform the look of art from the 19th century ideas of looking to nature as a reference to the radical world of 20th century abstraction and distortion. His goal was to make Impressionism more solid like the work of the old masters. The opposite effect was achieved. His brushwork and use of intensified color inspired Picasso to disassemble nature into cubes and Matisse to use large patches of solid color. The saying that Cézanne "is the father of us all" is attributed to Picasso and Matisse. This meant that Cézanne's art was the major influence in the art they created. He was not a social man. He preferred to work alone and study nearby scenes including Monte Sainte-Victoire, a mountain that appears in many of his landscapes. He set up carefully arranged still-life objects on small tables. To get the best angle for each item he tilted the pots and fruit up with items hid underneath the draperies and tablecloths. In this way, he created natural distortion of the view. Later artists would purposefully distort objects, as we see in the movement called Cubism.

The Challenge

Oil pastels will be used in the last eight units. They have an oily binder. They cannot be used with other types of pastels effectively. Sharpen oil pastels before you begin. Look for a pencil or crayon sharpener that has a large hole. Peel back the paper on the pastel stick and carefully turn until it comes to a point. The point will wear down quickly while you use the pastel. In order to make it last longer, rotate the pastel every few seconds as you work.

USING OIL PASTELS

In the illustration, you can see how the pastel touches the paper. For line work, hold the tip to the paper. To cover broader areas, lower the stick so that the side touches the paper. Blending is best accomplished by rubbing one color over another to make a heavy layer. Oil pastels do NOT need to be fixed or sprayed when finished. The oil in the pastel fixes it to the paper. The surface is delicate so take care when storing or displaying the picture.

Draw a picture of an object within your home with oil pastels. Choose an object that interests you.

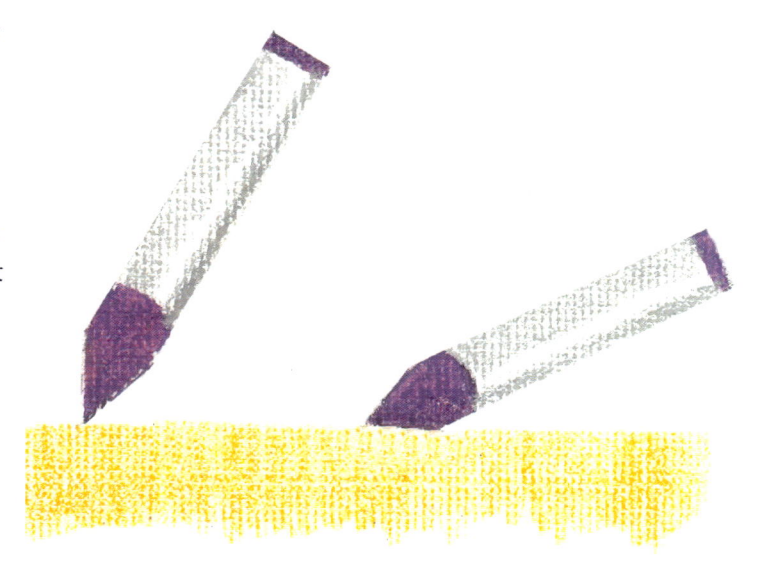

HOW TO BLEND USING OIL PASTELS

An oil pastel can be sharpened when you want to make a line. A worn, rounded edge is not easily controlled. Keep pastels sharp by rotating the pastel stick in your hand every few seconds as you draw. Held at the correct angle, the pastels will stay sharp. When one wears down, simply sharpen it again. Sharpeners like the one below have an opening for regular size pencils and for crayons or pastels.

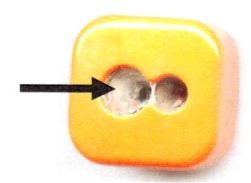 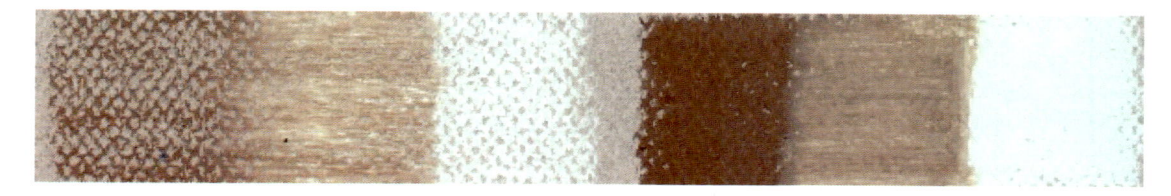

LIGHT PRESSURE   HEAVY PRESSURE

Oil pastels can be used lightly so that the color of the paper shows and becomes part of the picture or they can be used with a lot of pressure. Used with a lot of pressure, oil pastels can quickly fill up the indentations in the paper. When this happens, usually only two colors can be blended. A third color added simply slides off the surface, leaving no mark.

1. Use the point of the pastel to draw the outlines.

2. Use the side of the pastel to fill in spaces.

The gray paper works well as a shadow for the white cup. It is also seen in the background.

Try New Techniques

Choose a still-life object from your home. Choose a background paper that will become part of the color in your object. Draw the outline, and then fill in areas using light pressure so that the background can be seen.

The Project

We sometimes blend because of the way we see light and shaded areas. Notice how an assortment of pastel tints are applied to the paper in lines and are then blended to show form.

Set up a still-life of two or three simple objects. Consider placement on the page so that the objects balance. Shadows can be used as a color to balance the picture as well. Draw with oil pastels, keeping the pastels sharp as you go. Blend colors using your finger.

Student Gallery

Artwork by Kayleen Minnig. This work balances because the light blue shadow is seen on both sides of the picture. Light coming from the right casts a shadow to the left of each object.

Materials

- oil pastels
- sharpener
- drawing paper

References

Choose still-life subjects from your bedroom. Find objects you like and that will look good together. You objects might include:

- a decorative pillow
- a clock
- a treasured box
- sports equipment
- a game controller
- shoes
- a purse
- a cap
- a hat
- a stuffed toy

LOOK BACK! How do the objects within your picture balance?

UNIT 10
parallel rhythm

Rhythm is the repeated use of color, line, value, texture, or shape within a work of art. Since the eye is quick to see the relationship of similar things, rhythm is a useful tool for carrying the eye across the picture. Parallel lines in both horizontal and vertical positions create rhythm in this drawing by Nathan Voss.

Be Creative

Life is full of visual information, but we can miss it when we do not purposefully engage in the act of observing. Artists are visually more in tune with their world than the person who has never spent time looking at things. As artists draw, they continually observe. Observation is a skill that is developed.

TRY IT: Do a 5-minute drawing that is from memory of something you have observed in the last 24 hours. Continue this exercise daily, for the next two weeks. If you continue this short practice, you will find that you are becoming more aware of the world you live in. Each day is filled with great visual information. See for yourself!

5-minute memory sketches will not have a lot of detail at first. As your memory skills improve so will the amount of detail in your sketches. Here is a great sketch by student, Nathan Voss after working in this manner for about six months.

OBJECTIVE: to start a daily drawing habit that will greatly increase awareness of the visual material.

Look at Parallel Rhythm

Rhythm in a work of art is a repeated element of art: line, texture, shape, form, value, or color. It is like a repeating beat in music. Just as rhythms in music can be quite different and affect how we feel when listening, the rhythms in art can also be quite different. A rhythm creates a steady flow across the painting. These are controlled movements used to direct our eyes over a work of art and control the speed at which they travel. Here the artist uses vertical and diagonal lines. We feel a quiet, rhythmic calm as we look at this painting. Looking out over the bridge, the man sees another bridge. This was made during the industrial age and bridges were a monument to invention and man's ability to control nature. This made them worthy subjects for painting.

Gustave Caillebotte, *Le pont de l'Europe*, 1877.
Photo Credit : Dover Publications Inc.

Vertical lines are shown in blue.
Diagonal lines are shown in green.

The Artist

Gustave Caillebotte (1848-1894)
French Impressionist Painter and Collector

Caillebotte studied art at the French Academy after obtaining his law degree and fighting in the Franco-Prussian War. He became friends with artists outside the Academy, the Impressionists, and did much to help them in their struggles to get their work seen. He helped keep the group together with his diplomatic skills during disagreements. Because he was from a wealthy family, Caillebotte was able to help many Impressionists financially. He rented their exhibition space with his own money. He paid to advertise for the show, bought frames, and hung the pictures. He also made many of the first purchases and at his death donated sixty-eight Impressionist works to the French government. Without his management and marketing skills and his wealth it is questionable whether the Impressionists could have made such a bold impact in such a short time. They were known and their work accepted by the general public after just twelve years. Caillebotte was a painter as well as patron. His other interests included stamp collecting, gardening, and yachting.

The Challenge

Using hatch strokes is a way of creating texture on the picture space. Use any type of repeated motion with your hand to create other kinds of textures. Try making short dashes, dots, vertical lines, or using a tight wandering line. Some examples are shown below. How do the strokes change the appearance of the apple? Choose one simple object to explore texture. Draw it four or more times using different types of strokes each time.

| Dashes | Dots | Lines | Squiggles |

HOW TO MAKE HATCH STROKES

Hatching is to make quick lines that go in the same direction, and then to layer colors on top of each other. It is not like blending because each mark is distinct, and not blended into another. Here are some examples of hatch strokes in different colors. Hatching is a good technique to use with oil pastels because they do not blend as easily as soft pastels.

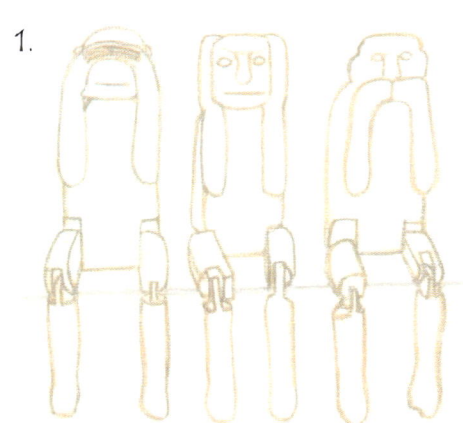

1. Begin by drawing the outline of the subjects you've chosen like the three monkeys shown on the left.

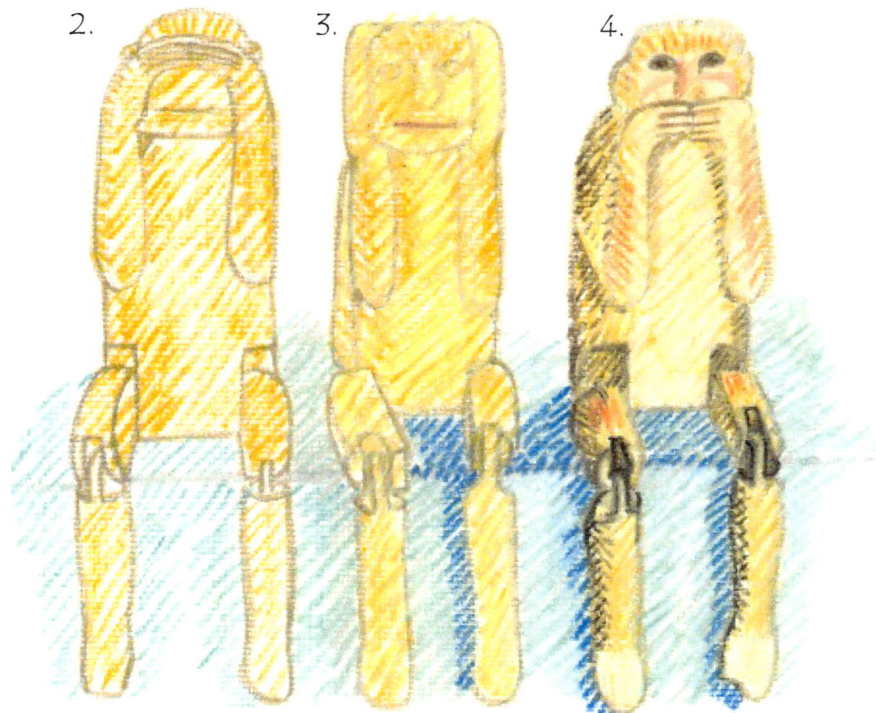

2. Put in the first layer of colors, which are the middle values, making your marks go in the same direction.

3. Add new colors, which are close to the middle values in the same strokes.

4. Finish by hatching in the very darkest and the very lightest areas.

Try New Techniques

Choose an object and try making hatch strokes as described above. Always choose subject matter that you like. Consider models, toys, sports equipment, favorite bedroom accessories, and things that are around you.

The Project

The monkeys on the previous page show rhythm through repetition of a similar form. They all have the same blockish shape. Look for this kind of repetition in a landscape scene.

Student Gallery

Student work by Annie Walker. This work uses blending throughout. Oil pastels were rubbed with her finger. Blending creates a calm mood. She creates rhythm with the parallel lines of the trees and their shapes.

Student work by Eva Fan. Eva created this work using a hatch stroke throughout the drawing. She creates rhythm in the curved lines following the edges of the water on both sides.

Materials

- oil pastels
- sharpener
- drawing paper
- drawing board

References

Go outdoors and look for rhythm. There are often rhythms to be found in manufactured things like buildings or along streets. Look in the following places:

- Flowerbeds
- Gardens
- Parks
- Roadsides
- Decks
- Lanes
- Fields
- Hedges
- Lakesides
- Home developments

LOOK BACK! Did you use the repetition of a subject to create rhythm in your work of art?

UNIT 11
converging rhythm

When lines converge or come together at a center point, it sets up a rhythm in the picture. In this work by Nathan Voss, the point lies a bit to the right of the top of the stool. The counter lines and booth lines converge to that point.

Be Creative

Creativity grows when you give time to it. It grows when you have the freedom to explore without feeling that someone will criticize your efforts. It grows when you have a reason to create. There needs to be something inside you that pushes you to find answers. Marcel Proust, (1871-1922), a French Novelist, states, "The real voyage of discovery consists not in seeking new landscapes but in having new eyes." He is saying that we do not have to travel to distant lands to see beautiful things but that wonders are all around us if we have eyes to see them.

TRY IT: Take a mini-trip through your neighborhood or a nearby area. Take time to look. Take time to make new discoveries. Feel the freedom to absorb the sights, the sounds, and the feel of the place. Afterward record some of your discoveries in a sketch.

OBJECTIVE: to give creativity a chance to work through time spent in observation of the natural world.

Look at Converging Rhythm

We are used to composing our pictures using either vertical or horizontal lines. Here the artist has used diagonal lines that converge or come together at the lower center of the painting. This unusual view creates a more dynamic scene. The man sits in the midst of piles of books and yet seems content as he holds his cat.

Edouard Vuillard, *Portrait of Theodore Duret*, 1912. Photo Credit: Dover Publications Inc.

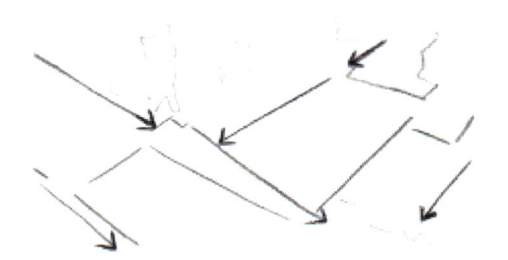

The diagonal lines created by the desk and stacks of papers converge toward the lower center of the painting.

61

The Culture

WORLD TRADE INFLUENCES ART OF EUROPE

In the Middle Ages, young European men wanting to be artists would work for a master painter for free as they gained skills. They were apprenticed. The medieval tradition of gaining skill through apprenticeships had developed into established schools of art by the 16th century. An artist would be trained in the techniques of the professors at the Art Academy. The Impressionists were all trained in this manner and yet they chose to consider the artistic techniques of a foreign nation. The Impressionists of the late 19th century set the tone for a new way of learning. An opening of world trade brought about this change. Nations that had been isolated before this time began to trade goods with one another and their art influenced the artists in distant places. In the late 19th century, textiles and other goods were being exported from Japan and other parts of the world. Japanese prints were so plentiful in Japan at the time that these goods were often wrapped in the prints, used as wrapping paper. The Impressionists were very interested by these new kinds of images. They discovered simple flat shapes and new compositional principles through these images. Impressionists collected Japanese prints and began incorporating these new ideas into their work. The Art Academies lost in the battle for influence and artists from this point on would be influenced by art from around the world. Within the next generation, Europeans like Gauguin would travel to Tahiti and Picasso would find influences in African tribal masks.

The Challenge

Color Families

Color families are groups of hues that have one color name such as "blue". There may be many variations within one family. When working in broken hues, as you will on the next page, you will want the picture to hold together visually. Do that by working within the same family of hues in specific areas. The plant on the next page was made by working within the green family. The background is primarily in the blue family.

Using your set of pastels, create a chart of hue family groups as shown above.

HOW TO DRAW IN BROKEN COLOR

Broken color is a technique developed by many Impressionist painters, especially Monet. The color is laid down in spots or dashes using short strokes. In the example shown here the strokes are as thick as the pastel end. The point will wear down quickly when using this method.

1. With a point, draw in the basic shapes.

2. Use color families within specific areas. The strokes should be as wide as the dulled end of a pastel.

3. There is very little overlapping of color in this method. Change colors often and allow colors to bump up next to each other. This picture was finished with black outlines around the leaves. Add black outlines if the object needs to be emphasized.

Try New Techniques

Choose an object or scene. Use broken color in a work of art. It is best if the subject is kept simple and has clearly defined edges. Work on any color of background that you prefer. Here the artist chose white paper.

1.

2.

3.

The Project

Create a picture using converging rhythm. The composition should radiate out from a given point. While looking down upon a plant, you will usually notice this effect. When coloring the picture, use colors within the same color families, rather than just one color. For instance, a sky could contain all the colors within the blue color family, rather than one hue.

Student Gallery

This student work is by Laurel Ellis. The lines made by the animal's bodies converge.

Materials

- oil pastels
- sharpener
- drawing paper

References

Look for still life objects or a landscape scene that has converging rhythm. You may find this kind of rhythm in the following places:

- A flower
- A plant
- A spiraling staircase
- A group of couches arranged around a room.
- An open umbrella

LOOK BACK! Does the composition within you picture seem to radiate out from a given point, showing converging rhythm?

UNIT 12
space with little depth

Look at the backgrounds chosen for these two portraits. The first is after a painting by Kahlo, shown on the next page. The second is after a work titled *Mona Lisa* by Leonardo da Vinci. Kahlo creates a space with little depth bringing leaves close up behind the portrait. Leonardo da Vinci creates extreme depth showing distant mountains, trees, and roadways.

little depth   extreme depth

Be Creative

"Composition is the art of arranging in a decorative manner the various elements at the painter's disposal for the expression of his feelings." –Henry Matisse, artist. Matisse states that art is more than a representation of how something looks. It is a representation of the artists feelings as well. What kinds of things affect the look of a specific scene? Circumstances or your mood may affect how you feel about the scene. The time of year, the time of day, or the weather may affect how it actually looks. You may simply feel like making different kinds of marks to describe it at different times. All these things determine how an artist treats a work of art. Many artists return to the same scene or subject for years, painting it in a new way each time.

TRY IT: Choose a scene that is located outdoors, subject to weather, lighting, or other physical changes. Draw or paint it today in a way that you feel shows the mood. Return to it at different times and with different mediums. If you let yourself be affected each time, you will never paint the same picture twice!

CREATIVE CORY

Face it, Cory. It's the only view of old Bessie that you haven't drawn yet.

OBJECTIVE: to understand that it is not the subject, but the artist's interpretation of the subject that makes interesting art.

Look at Space with Little Depth

Frida Kahlo, *Self-Portrait with Monkey*, 1938. Photo Credit: Dover Publications Inc.

Sometimes we cannot see back into a picture very far. Here the artist has painted a self-portrait. The small monkey sits directly behind her. The background of leaves and foliage is very near the back of her head. The close up view of the leaves allows us to see their delicate textures. This texture adds interest to the picture. Since the view is about the artist and her pet, there is no need to show further details by including something in the distance.

Depth is shown by what is in the background. The background is colored in this diagram. The face is not the background.

The Artist

Frida Kahlo (1907 –1954)
Mexican painter

Frida Kahlo used vibrant colors in paintings, which were influenced by the indigenous cultures of Mexico and European styles. She made mostly self-portraits that incorporated real physical existence and spiritual elements. She was the victim of a traffic accident early in life and underwent many operations. Her acute awareness of her body and the pain she dealt with constantly, were the subjects for most of her artwork. Her paintings often show internal body parts. The surrealists thought she was one of them. They placed bizarre and unrelated objects together to create confusion in people's minds. However, Kahlo's artwork simply reflected her Mexican heritage. The people of Mexico had always created art that combined the physical world with the spiritual world. They had no trouble placing a demon or saint in the corner of a painting alongside the people going about their daily lives. Kahlo was not inventing as the Surrealists, but following the traditions of her people as she painted her own reality of what was happening outside her body and within it.

The Culture

MEXICAN ART TRADITION

Our ideas of art today are greatly influenced by the four-hundred years (1500-1900) in which Europeans focused on the physical world by representing what they saw in the most realistic way that they could. Separating this physical reality from spiritual reality was a European invention. It was at odds with the way many cultures, including the Indian tribes in Mexico, perceived the world. Even Europeans had understood this spiritual context and included it in their art in the past. For fourteen-hundred years (100-1500) religious art, created in Europe, placed angels, saints, demons, and other spirit beings alongside images of people who dwelled on the earth. Native North and South American tribes painted and carved spirits in human and animal form. When European spirituality was introduced to tribes in Mexico, a mixture of Catholic and native imagery placed people in a world filled with spiritual beings, both good and evil. The art of Mexico today is a brightly colored mixture of ancient Indian lore and Spanish colonial traditions including woodcarving, pottery, dolls, weavings, and paintings.

The Challenge

We see surface pattern and texture in the background of the painting by Kahlo. You can make surface pattern by carefully copying lines and patterns that you see on objects or you can use a technique called rubbing or frottage. Play around with different textured surfaces. Lay textured objects on a table surface. Arrange the objects in a pleasing manner. Lay a piece of lightweight drawing paper over the objects. Rub the end or side of the pastel over the paper with moderate pressure until the surface texture shows up on the paper. See the next page for a visual example.

HOW TO USE FROTTAGE

Frottage is a technique using a textured surface and rubbing the pastel stick over the paper. Variations in the textured surface are transferred onto the paper. The effects of frottage are as unique as the surfaces that you rub.

Draw a picture in lines only, onto lightweight drawing paper. Do not use pastel paper. It is too thick.

To create the texture, place your paper over a textured surface such as a cardboard box, doily, screen, stucco wall, brick, rough textured concrete or rough wood paneling. Rub the oil pastel back and forth gently over the paper. The textured surface will work with the softness of the pastel and dark and light areas will be transferred onto the paper. Experiment on a scrap sheet of paper before putting it into the picture. The results are often surprising and unexpected.

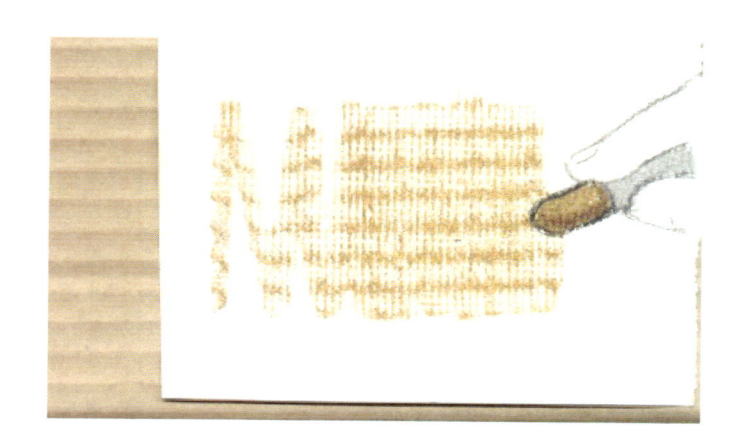

Shown here is a work of art inspired by a pizza. The cardboard pizza box was used to create the textured surface of the pizza box in the picture. A doily was not available for the tablecloth, so a raised pattern on a flowerpot was used. The pizza was colored in without the use of frottage.

Try New Techniques

On a thin piece of paper (drawing or copy paper) use frottage to see what types of marks are possible with the different textures that you find. Create a picture using some of those textures. Sometimes a texture can inspire the subject for the picture, as the pizza box did in the work above.

The Project

Do not think that you have to look far for a textured surface for frottage. You can create your own textured surface with thick paper like pastel paper. Below are the results of rubbing the pastel over paper cutouts. Thick paper is cut and woven in the first example. A snowflake is cut from paper in the second example. Paper cutouts were placed under a thinner sheet of paper such as drawing or charcoal paper. The pastel was then rubbed over the surface of the paper.

Materials

- oil pastels
- sharpener
- heavy paper like pastel paper
- Lightweight paper like drawing, copy, or charcoal paper
- scissors

Student Gallery

Draw a picture from your imagination using oil pastel. You can refer to pictures or real life to gather information for your colored drawing. Think how you will show that one object sits in front of another. Create a picture with little depth. Use frottage in some area of the picture.

Student work by Laurel Ellis. The frottage technique was used for the texture of the trees.

References

Make up a scene from your imagination. Use your observations of real life as inspiration.

LOOK BACK! Did you show little depth within the picture and use frottage as a means of creating a textured surface?

The Elements Combined- Color and Texture

1.

2.

3.

Oil pastels can be used to create smooth textures as well as rough textures. Choose a subject to draw that has both types of textures. Set up a still-life of two or three objects with shinny surfaces. Outline the subjects of your still-life using a light color. 1. The shinny surface of frosting was created by layering thickly with oil pastels. The first layer was dark brown. The darkest areas were covered with black. Rust was added on top. White was used over brown for the highlights. 2. Turn the paper as needed so that you can pull smooth strokes. Here the blue pastel is used on its side and carefully drawn up against the edge of the napkin. 3. White is used on its side over the blue to blend. It was not placed on as thickly as the frosting area, so that the surface retains its rough texture. The finished work shows both very rough textures cause by the surface of drawing paper and shinny surfaces created by overlapping colors and applying them thickly. Gently tap the paper to knock off pieces of oil pastel. Do not rub the surface with your hand or the work may smear.

UNIT 13
depth

People in different times and different locations have developed different ways of showing depth on a flat surface. One way is to overlap objects. A second way is to decrease the size of the object while raising it on the picture plane. A third way is to raise the more distant object on the picture plane either above or to the side of the nearer object without changing size. In the drawing at the right, Nathan Voss uses the second method of showing depth. Objects rise on the picture plane as they go into the distance and decrease in size as well.

1.   2.   3.

Be Creative

Art can reflect the character of the things it describes. Imagine two different shoes, one old and one new. With the old shoe, emphasis could be made by showing a worn out toe, bent heal, broken strap, or deep creases in the leather. In contrast, emphasis on the new shoe could focus on the shiny surface and clean edges.

TRY IT: Find a subject in which you can observe old and new. This might be shoes or an old toothpaste tube and a new one. Draw one subject showing old and new within the same drawing. Emphasize the qualities that make the old one look old and the qualities that make the new one look new.

OBJECTIVE: to think about the character of the subject and how one might interpret those characteristics in an artwork.

CREATIVE CORY

Really, Cory, some old things ought to be disposed of, not drawn.

Look at Depth in Art

In this painting, we see the way the study of depth developed in Europe after the Middle Ages. The man overlaps the tree he leans on showing he is in front of it. As they go into the distance, the position of the men rises on the page. The further in the distance they are, the smaller the figures become. Look for the signs of depth (shown below) in the painting.

Frederic Bazille, *Summer Scene,* 1869.
Photo Credit: Dover Publications Inc.

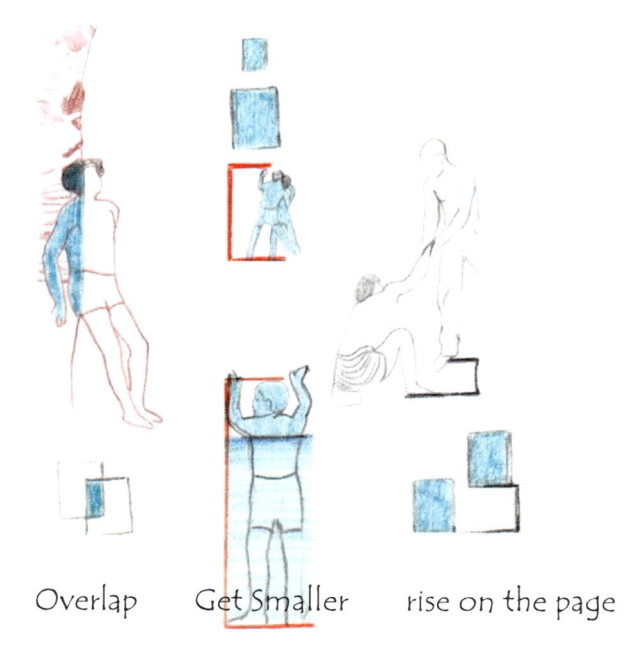

Overlap   Get Smaller   rise on the page

In the painting above, we see all these ways of showing depth.

The Artist

Jean Frédéric Bazille
(1841-1870)
French Impressionist Painter

As a young man, Bazille studied art and began to produce art along with Manet, Monet, and Sisley. He came from a wealthy family. He offered his artist friends space in his studio to work and materials to paint with. His works were created in his twenties. At age twenty-nine Frédéric Bazille joined a regiment in the Franco-Prussian War. He died in action the same year.

The Culture

SUPPORTERS OF THE ARTS

Artists have always needed supporters, those who would purchase their works or who supported them as they worked. In the Middle Ages, art was largely created by Monks who had protection in monasteries and supported themselves as a large group, growing their own crops for food. The Renaissance period and afterward was a period where artists were hired and housed by wealthy patrons, usually rulers, kings, or bishops. They created the works that the patron requested. In the 19th century, artists began making works that related to their own interests. If these were not in demand by wealthy individuals, an artist could starve. Both Bazille and Caillebotte helped the experimental Impressionists by purchasing their works and buying supplies for them until their works were accepted and wanted by the public. The history of art may have taken a different turn without the support of these two men.

The Challenge

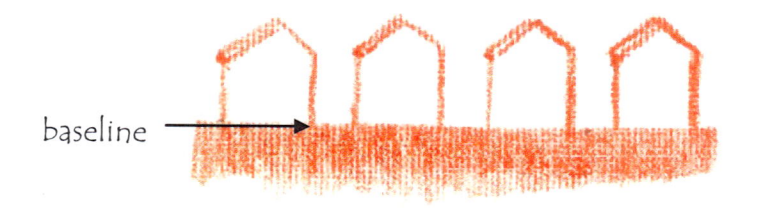

baseline →

These houses sit on four baselines, rising as they go into the distance.

Objects of the same size will appear to be the same distance from the viewer if they are drawn the same size and on the same baseline.

When drawn in decreasing sizes, they appear to be further in the distance. When drawn on a baseline that gets higher on the picture plane, they appear to be further in the distance.

Using warm colors (yellows, orange, and reds) in the foreground and cooler colors (blues, purples, greens) in the background will imply distance.

Look outdoors for repeated objects that go into the distance. They could be trees, houses, or posts. Draw a scene using the information shown here for creating the look of distance.

HOW TO BLOCK IN COLORS

Blocking in is what happens in the middle step of a three step color drawing. **1.** The first step is to draw the lines that describe what you see. To draw lines, you should use the tip of a sharpened oil pastel.

2. Next, block in large areas of similar color or value. When blocking in, look for large areas of distinct colors in what you are observing. Overlook the details while you work in this stage of the drawing. To block in large areas of color you should use the side of a pointed pastel to cover more area. **3.** The final step is to layer colors over the areas you have blocked in. You can use the same color, adding extra layers to make the picture more intense. You can use different colors, layering them for a blended effect.

1.

2.

3.

Try New Techniques

Draw a landscape in color using colored paper and the three steps shown on this page. Work outdoors if possible or find a view from a window. Block in colors in the second step.

74

The Project

Show depth in a picture using oil pastels. Apply the rules for distance as shown on page 72. Apply the techniques shown on page 74.

Student Gallery

Student work is by Matthew Smaldone. Matthew noticed large shapes defined by their color. He blocked in the areas of color. Instead of individual tree shapes, he shows the shape of the tree mass. He blocks in dark blue mountain peaks and a white shape to define the area of snow. The picture has a beautiful feel because of the large, clearly defined shapes.

Materials

- oil pastels
- sharpener
- pastel paper or drawing paper
- drawing board

References

Look at a landscape while working. Show objects that are of interest to you. Choose what will be in the picture and what will not. Landscapes are often full of too much information and you should choose only the most outstanding features for your drawing.

LOOK BACK! Did you create a sense of depth by overlapping objects or decreasing the size of objects while raising them on the picture plane? Did you imply distance in any other ways?

UNIT 14
VIEWPOINT
HIGH

Viewpoint is the point that marks the eye level of the artist in relation to the subject. To get a high point of view the artist's eye level needs to be higher than the subject is. A high viewpoint allows you to show what is happening on the ground or under the object with a wide view of that area.

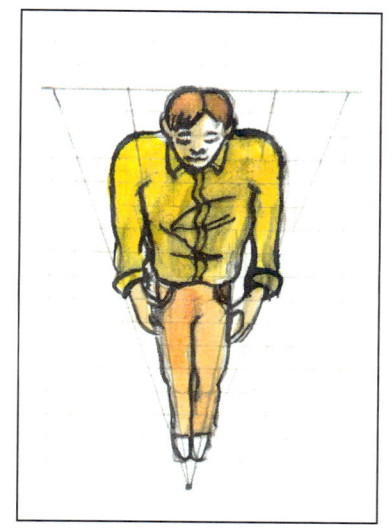

Be Creative

Unity is a quality about a work of art that pulls it together. Many artists have unique brush strokes, which are the unifying part of their work. For example, the short parallel strokes used by Cézanne or light wispy strokes used by Mary Cassatt are the mark of their work. One can also achieve unity using a type of line predominately. One might emphasize a color, giving a painting a bluish or yellowish hue throughout. Look at a selection of your own work. What makes it unique? What quality is used throughout the work? It could be that you use heavy, dark marks. It could be that you concentrate on the surfaces, making the work very textural.

TRY IT: Decide what unifying qualities already exist in your work and emphasize them further in a new work of art. If you cannot find a unifying quality, then choose an element such as texture and create unity by emphasizing that.

OBJECTIVE: to help the student to discover the strengths in their own work at present and give understanding on how an artist pushes toward a mark or goal to accomplish a more personal feel to their work.

CREATIVE CORY

CORY TAKES A HIGH VIEWPOINT

76

Look at High Viewpoint in Art

A high point of view gives the viewer the advantage of seeing more of the action. It is the same as being in a stadium, sitting high above the players. To create a scene like this, the artist must be higher than the figures. In this work of art, a high point of view seems especially appropriate because we are looking at an intimate scene inside the dwelling of a couple as they hold their child. They sit on leopard skins and are accompanied by Hindu deities in the form of animals. The figures at the bottom of the painting seem to be below the couple. We feel as if we are looking down on them.

Unknown Artist, Shiva and Pavati surrounded by most of the Hindu deities:
19th c. Photo Credit: Dover Publications Inc., NY

The rock formations make an interesting pattern within the painting and separate the couple from the figures below as well as tie the whole picture together in a type of figure 8. Notice the details of birds and leaves, which are common to these intricate small paintings designed for manuscripts.

The Art

ILLUMINATED MANUSCRIPTS

Little is written about individual artists who painted the illuminated manuscripts for Middle Eastern Kings. They were considered craftsmen and worked in the courts of the sultans. Pictures like these are brightly colored detailed illustrations for books. Scenes depicted love, life of the courts, and battles. Many, like this one, were shown with a high point of view so the details are seen clearly. These illustrated books, also called illuminated manuscripts, were a mixture of historical fact and fiction. Akbar was a supporter of Persian artists and directed an academy of local painters during his reign. The paintings of illuminated manuscripts show Indian tastes in bright colors and perfection of details in costumed figures, animals and backgrounds. The paintings are usually identified by the school from which they were produced.

The Culture

ROYAL PATRONAGE OF THE ARTS IN IRAN

The arts thrive on the patronage of those with wealth. For many centuries, art was not a part of the common person's experience. Art was for royalty. A patron is one who supports artists financially by commissioning them for a work or providing a salary. Schools of art in Persia were under the patronage of the Shahs of Iran. The Safavid period from 1500-1722 produced many Persian miniature paintings. The art depicts the life and activities of the patrons. Figures became more individualized and showed gestures and expressions that are more realistic during this time. Traditionally painting was thought to serve the purpose of enhancing the text of poetry and literature. Most Iranian painting was created for book illustration. Rarely did painting stand alone, except for portraits of Shahs, which hung in their palaces. The portraits were made after the tradition of European portraits of Kings. They are European in the style of painting and have little to do with the Persian tradition of art as book illustration.

The Challenge

We usually look at objects from a side view with the artist being at the same level as the object. When the artist steps above the object, the artist has taken a high point of view. Find an object and place yourself above it. Draw the object from a high point of view. Think of subjects that might look good from this view. Drawing what is inside a fruit bowl, a laundry basket, or toy bin might make an interesting work of art.

HOW TO USE MASKING

Masking is a way to create clearly defined edges. A mask is a paper that protects the surface of the picture in areas that you do not want to draw onto. You can outline shapes that you fill in with color. Cut the shape out of regular paper and hold it down on the picture surface while you apply the color.

To make a mask, draw the shapes that you wish to color. Cut out the shapes by poking a hole in the middle of each shape with a scissors, and then cutting to the line and around the line. You can use a mask repeatedly as shown below.

Six stone-like shapes are cut out of paper to make a mask. The mask is placed over a sheet of paper. The cut out area of the mask is colored into, using several colors for each stone. The mask is then moved and colored repeatedly until the stones fill the picture.

The mask is then set aside. The artist colors in the flower. The black area between the stones is filled in to finish the work.

Try New Techniques

Cut a mask of an object that can be repeated like stones, leaves, bricks, blades of grass, etc. Finish a picture using the mask as shown above.

The Project

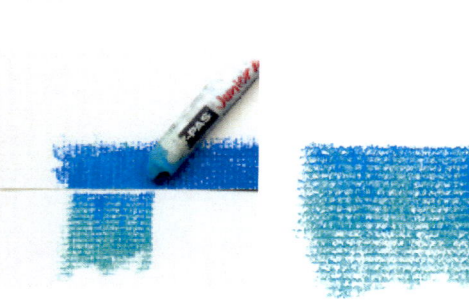

MASKS

To pull a straight edge without a line, you can use a scrap sheet of paper to mask an area. Lay the straight edge where you want the edge to be. Using pastel, draw from the scrap paper onto the picture. When you lift the scrap sheet, the edge will be straight. To layer colors, lay down a heavy layer of color on the edge of the scrap sheet. With a different color, draw from the scrap paper onto the picture, pulling the top layer into the picture.

Materials

- oil pastels
- sharpener
- pastel paper or drawing paper
- scissors
- extra paper for a mask
- scissors

Student Gallery

Color a picture that shows a high point of view. You would be looking down on the subject. Many still-life artists find that their subjects are more interesting when looking down on them. Try it.

Student work is by Laurel Ellis. Here the student cut a mask for the kitten figure. The blanket was then drawn around the kitten.

References

Set up a still life subject. Look for interesting objects in

- shelves
- toy boxes
- your room
- a sibling's room

LOOK BACK! Did you show a high point of view and use a mask while making your picture?

UNIT 15
viewpoint
LOW

Viewpoint is the point that marks the eye level of the artist in relation to the subject. To get a low point of view, the artist's eye level needs to be lower than the subject is. A low viewpoint makes the object look massive, gigantic, or impressive.

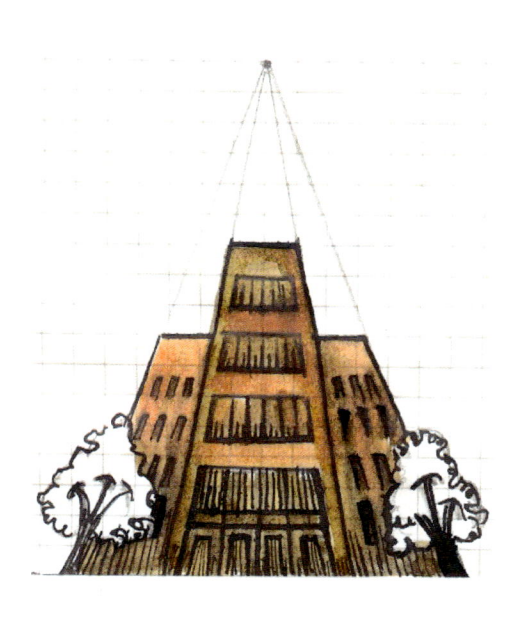

Be Creative

Use variety in art to create interest. People lose interest in a work quickly when too many parts of it look the same. Variety is shown in the parts of the work that vary or that are different from other parts. One can create variety by contrasting the smoothness of a sky with the rough texture of the leaves shown against it. Observe this in the painting on the next page. One might create variety in their choice of colors. If a painting or drawing is light in value, one should create variety by adding darker values in some parts of the work.

TRY IT: Look at a work of art you've done in the past. Choose a work that does not have much variety and decide how it could be improved. Make the changes on the work itself or do another similar work, this time adding variety to it.

OBJECTIVE: to create an awareness of variety in art works and to begin to evaluate one's own work to make it better.

Look at Low Viewpoint in Art

In a low point of view, the artist positions himself or herself below the main object in the artwork. In a landscape, the viewer would see a lot of sky within the picture because the viewer is looking up. The horizon is low within the picture space. The viewer looks up to the paper lanterns, to the tree branches, and to the rooftop in this woodcut by Hiroshige.

Hiroshige, Evening Cherry at Nakanocho in the Yoshiwara, c. 1834–35.
Photo Credit: Dover Publications Inc.

In a low point of view, more sky in seen and less ground.

The Artist

Utagawa Hiroshige (1797-1858), Japanese Woodblock artist

Hiroshige's father was a firefighter for the castle of Edo and he lived with his family and thirty other samurai in ten barracks. Since their only duty was to fight fires, they had lots of time to pursue other activities. Painting was one of them. Hiroshige grew up and studied as an artist. He went on a long journey and painted what he saw on his travels. He produced a large group of prints featuring locations and tales of fellow travelers, along with details of the 490-kilometer (303 mile) trip. These were produced in 1833 and 1834. The prints feature travelers along famous routes and stops of special attractions and sites in Japan. They were painted in all kinds of weather: rain, snow, wind, and hail and during all of the seasons. These prints were very popular so he started on a second journey and produced prints of stops along the Edo Road. (1834-1842). He painted thousands of these small-scale works.

The Challenge

Draw a landscape from a low point of view. If you live near tall buildings, you might sit beneath them. Find a low point in the landscape where you can sit and observe something above.

A low point of view allows us to see more of the ceiling. The picture below gives us a look into the view a small child might have.

HOW TO USE RESIST WITH OIL PASTELS

Oil resists water. You can use oil pastels and any liquid water based color to create a resist. Lay down lines or patches of color using your oil pastels and then brush over the entire picture with a wash of ink or watercolor. Black or a dark color is preferable. The oil pastel marks repel the liquid and it settles around the marks, leaving the colors bright.

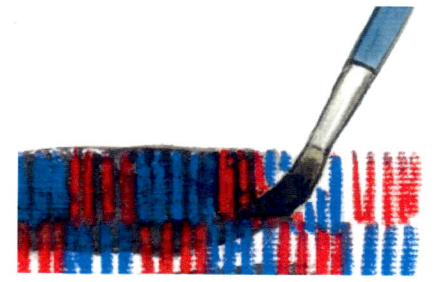

The red and blue stripes made in oil pastel, resist the thin black watercolor paint or ink.

As you draw, apply the pastel heavily. Any indentions in the paper that the oil pastel has not covered will become the color of the liquid paint that you use. Do leave some spaces without pastel so that the black color has somewhere to go.

Try New Techniques

Draw and color a picture using oil pastels.

Thin black watercolor or ink in a small dish or lid and brush over the entire sheet of paper as seen in the upper portion of this work. If too many pools of black obstruct the picture, you can dab them up with a paper towel.

The black will stick to any part of the paper that is not covered with oil pastel.

Think of a viewpoint that is low. Draw from that perspective in oil pastels. Apply the resist method using an ink or watercolor wash as described above.

The Project

Draw or paint a picture in pastel showing a low point of view. You may have to sit below a tall object or place an object above you. Try placing a box on a table as you sit at the table. If tall enough, this will raise the object above your eye-level as you sit and draw.

Student Gallery

This student work by Gemma Nowak was created by sitting below the birdhouse. She used the resist technique shown on the previous page.

Materials

- oil pastel
- paper
- sharpener
- watercolor or ink
- brush
- watercolor can
- paper towel

References

Draw from observation. Look up! The object might be one of the following:

- a kitchen appliance
- a stuffed toy
- a model
- a birdhouse
- a pot of plants
- a lamp
- a ceiling fan
- a weathervane

LOOK BACK! Did you draw from a low point of view? If so, what do we see in the top half of the picture?

UNIT 16
emphasis

To emphasize is to make a part of the picture stand out from the other parts. One can emphasize a specific object or objects by their placement. By placing three young men on a straight line that converges to the vanishing point, they become different in size. The young man in front is bigger and so emphasis is given to him.

Be Creative

Perhaps you've heard that some people are naturally creative and some are not. You may be wondering which type you are. Before deciding, answer this: Can a plant grow without roots, stem, leaves, or flowers? Most people will answer "no" because of the way they think about plants. The answer is that a plant can grow without roots, stem, leaves, and flowers when it is designed to do so, like the fungus types of plants. In the same way the word "plant" has been defined too narrowly, so has the word "creativity". People are designed to be creative. The ability to put together ideas and thoughts that are your own is part of being human. Begin to take risks in the arts. Some things may fail. However, other things may work. As you decide you can take risks in the arts, you can then gain confidence to take the risks of being creative in other areas of your life. It's a lot of fun!

TRY IT: Look through books on paintings and try a new way of working that you admire. Look at topics like Impressionism, the Mughal School, Japanese prints, or Celtic patterns. Take a risk and try something new. Make a work of art in color in one of the style you chose. You are being creative when you do!

OBJECTIVE: to encourage creativity through gathering new information and using it in the student's own work, dispelling the idea that this activity is "copying" and therefore uncreative.

Lesson 2 # Look at Emphasis in Art

The Book of Kells c. 800 A.D./ Iona Island/ 330 x 241 mm/ Folio 7 verso Photo Credit: Dover Publications Inc. NY

This is a single page from a book created by Celtic Monks in 800 AD. The scene depicts the Virgin Mary seated on a throne, holding the infant Christ and surrounded by angels. We see the Celtic influence in the design of the border. Intricately woven patterns curve and twist around each other. These patterns, knots, and spirals often morph into animal heads, legs, or other body parts. Notice the head of a lion and the head of a bird, circled on the close up of the border. This border emphasizes the main figure because it surrounds her. When we look closer, an x is formed by the figures in the corners and the additions to the outside corners of the border (green), with Mary and Christ centered within it. The Celtic tradition was extremely aware of using intricate patterns to give emphasis to a figure through arrangement of the patterns.

The Culture

CELTIC ART

The Celts were a diverse group of independent, indigenous tribal societies. While similarities in language, artifacts, religion, and social structures are known, each culture had its own language and traditions" (Frost). Following the fall of the Roman Empire, a great many Celts from the North made their homes throughout Europe. They brought with them a type of art that was decorative and had a function when fighting battles. These art objects offered protection and scared off enemies. Their images were unique and lasting. Dragons, demons, twisted animal figures, birds and men were pounded into metal, carved into their sledges and ships, and later, painted into intricate borders surrounding images of the new Christian religion they adopted. Gombrich states that, "There are reasons for believing that they…thought of such images as a means of working magic and exorcizing evil spirits… There were laws among the Norwegian Vikings, which required the captain of a ship to remove these figures before entering his home port, 'so as not to frighten the spirits of the land' (Gombrich 120). Romans called the newcomers "Barbarians," a negative term, because they destroyed Roman and Greek art as they conquered and pillaged their lands. While the art of Europe would eventually develop to inspire, instruct, and be admired objects of beauty, Celtic art of the Dark Ages had a more practical reason to be created. Art has many purposes and expresses the beliefs and ideas of the people who create it. Because it uses imagery that we can all relate to, art often becomes a bridge for one culture to identify with another. While different languages pose a barrier to communication, art stands alone as a way for people to understand each other.

The Challenge

This project will be made up entirely of lines. The goal is to simplify an animal figure, reducing it to line and shape only. Like Celtic art, draw outlines around head, thigh, and torso. Fill the body shapes with color. This work is by Laurel Ellis, 2012.

HOW TO Design Celtic Ornamentation

Spirals, step patterns, and key patterns are found in Celtic art before the Celts incorporated Christian images in 450's A.D. The artwork contained images from life, such as animals, plants, and humans. Notice in the top row the knots of yellow and orange loop over each other and that the pattern is repeated.

In the second row, a head at one end and a tail at the other are joined, creating a heart shape. This shape is flipped and overlaps to join eight of these shapes. The colors are flipped as well, creating an intricate and complex pattern. By observing the complex patterns you can come up with patterns of your own.

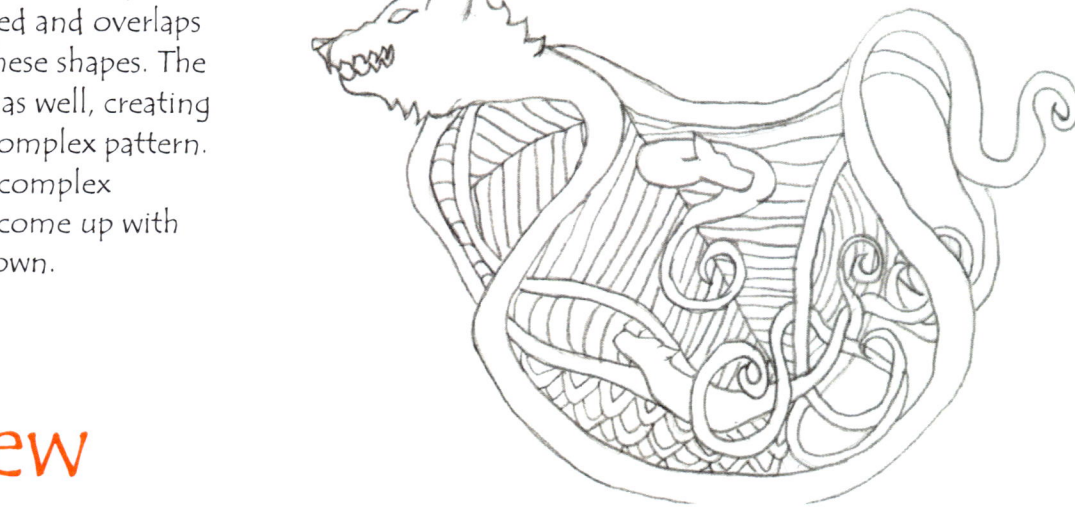

1.

Try New Techniques

1. Draw a Celtic knot design in pencil. Overlap the forms. You may want to make a continuous knot, one in which the ends are joined. The Celts often made this type of knot. Erase the extra lines as others overlap. Incorporate animal ornamentation into the design.

2. Add color by carefully filling in the shapes.

2.

The Project

Make your own Celtic design with emphasis as you study the detail below. Begin in pencil, and then finish with color pastels. Keep the pastels sharp for this project if your design requires detail. This design shows a pattern within a pattern. Draw a pattern or a figure and then emphasize it by placing a border around the central figure.

Materials

- Oil pastels
- Pencil
- Eraser
- White paper

References

Draw from a photograph of an:
- Animal
- Fish
- Bird
- Person

Use parts of these forms in your design or if you prefer, draw a pattern within a pattern. You can see more examples of Celtic knot designs on the internet.

Student Gallery

This image by Laurel Ellis shows emphasis by centering a simplified animal form within a complex knot design.

Evaluation Sheet
For Obtaining a Number and Letter Grade

Teachers may calculate a number and letter grade for each project within each unit. Follow the instructions below when reviewing the final work. DO NOT take off points for concepts not yet taught. Follow the objectives carefully when grading.

Because of the subjective qualities of art, it is best to mark higher rather than lower when deciding between two levels of achievement. If the student enjoys doing the lessons and has made the effort to create a work of art in a thoughtful way, then that student should be given a good grade. Allow the student to grow into mature artistic expression. Do not demand results that can only be obtained by years of experience that the student has not yet had. It is very likely that an individual who enjoys making art will get A's. This does not mean that the student has arrived at a full knowledge and use of artistic concepts. It does mean the student is doing well in the pursuit of that goal.

LEVELS OF ACHIEVEMENT: Choose the number of points that most accurately describes the work from each of the three categories below. Add the numbers from categories 1, 2, 3, and 4. This is the student's total score for the unit. This number can be translated into a letter grade: 90-100 (A), 80-89 (B), 70-79 (C), Uncompleted work (D-F).

1. Creative Exercise	2. The Challenge	3. Technique Drawing	4. The Project
25 POINTS/ COMPLETED ASSIGNMENT OBTAINING ALL OBJECTIVES IN THE BROWN BOX	25 POINTS/ COMPLETED ASSIGNMENT SHOWING GOOD UNDERSTANDING OF CONCEPT SHOWN IN ART WORK	25 POINTS/ COMPLETED ASSIGNMENT SHOWING A GOOD UNDERSTANDING AND USE OF MATERIALS OR TECHNIQUES	25 POINTS/ COMPLETED PROJECT SHOWING A GOOD UNDERSTANDING OF THE UNIT (SEE TITLE) AND USE OF THOSE ITEMS ASKED FOR IN THE BLACK BOX, AT THE BOTTOM OF THE PAGE
20 POINTS/ COMPLETED ASSIGNMENT OBTAINING SOME OF THE OBJECTIVES IN THE BROWN BOX	20 POINTS/ COMPLETED ASSIGNMENT SHOWING AN ATTEMPT TO USE CONCEPT SHOWN IN ART WORK	20 POINTS/ COMPLETED ASSIGNMENT SHOWING AN ATTEMPT TO USE MATERIALS OR TECHNIQUES	20 POINTS/ COMPLETED PROJECT SHOWING AN UNDERSTANDING OF THE UNIT BUT DID NOT ACCOMPLISH SOME ITEMS ASKED FOR IN THE BLACK BOX, AT THE BOTTOM OF THE PAGE
15 POINTS/ COMPLETED ASSIGNMENT BUT DID NOT OBTAIN OBJECTIVES IN THE BROWN BOX	15 POINTS/ COMPLETED ASSIGNMENT DID NOT USE CONCEPT SHOWN IN ART WORK	15 POINTS/ COMPLETED ASSIGNMENT DID NOT USE MATERIALS CORRECTLY OR TRY THE TECHNIQUES SHOWN	15 POINTS/ COMPLETED PROJECT DID NOT SHOW UNDERSTANDING OF THE UNIT OR ITEMS ASKED FOR IN THE BLACK BOX, AT THE BOTTOM OF THE PAGE

Note: If you do not see how the student accomplished the objectives asked for, do ask them about it. At times, the student will understand the objective very well and will be able to tell you how they accomplished the task in the drawing. This is valid. Remember that getting a visual idea across clearly is a process that takes time. Allow the student to grow it.

Bibliography

Gombrich, E.H., *The Story of Art*. Phaidon Press Inc., New York, NY, pocket edition 2006.

Janson, H.W. *History of Art, A Survey of the Major Visual Arts from the Dawn of History to the Present Day*. Prentice-Hall, Inc. Englewood Cliffs, N.J. and Harry N. Abrams, Inc., New York,

Frost, Martin. "Celt" http://www.martinfrost.ws/htmlfiles/gazette/celt.html. Retrieved Nov. 15, 2007.

Varnedoe, Kirk. *Odd Man In; A Brief Historiography of Caillebotte's Changing Roles in the History of Art*. www.artchive.com/artchive/C/caillebotte.html. Retrieved Jan. 17, 2008.

The Story of Art by E.H. Gombrich
Published by Phaidon Press Inc.

This book is a great introduction to the entire story of art from cave painting to the later part of the 20th century. Its short chapters and conversational manner make it easy to understand. The writing is simple. Gombrich does not use excessive wordiness. Here students and parents will get a concise, clearly organized narrative. Gombrich has incredible insight into human nature and makes connections so that we see art as a continual flow. Each artist takes part in the tradition of his time and Gombrich clearly points out what those traditions and mindsets were. Artwork also hints toward future developments as one work inspires new ideas for other artists. These connections give better understanding to human thought and Gombrich is not afraid to discuss the rich spiritual heritage that took hold in Europe from the medieval period through the Renaissance. Those art enthusiasts who would rather look than read will be pleased to know that over half of the book is devoted to pictures. This book should be a first choice for all newcomers to art.